GRAHAM GREENE AND THE HEART OF THE MATTER

TO MY FATHER AND MOTHER

Graham Greene
and the heart
of the matter

An essay by Marie-
Béatrice Mesnet

GREENWOOD PRESS, PUBLISHERS
WESTPORT, CONNECTICUT

The Library of Congress has catalogued this publication as follows:

Library of Congress Cataloging in Publication Data

Mesnet, Marie Béatrice.
    Graham Greene and the heart of the matter.

    Reprint of the 1954 ed.
    Bibliography: p.
    1. Greene, Graham, 1904-   I. Title.
PR6013.R44Z654 1972   823'.9'12   72-6404
ISBN 0-8371-6490-7

First published in 1954
by The Cresset Press, London

Reprinted with the permission
of Marie-Béatrice Mesnet

First Greenwood Reprinting 1972

Library of Congress Catalogue Card Number 72-6404

ISBN 0-8371-6490-7

Printed in the United States of America

ACKNOWLEDGMENTS

I wish to express my deep sense of gratitude to Mr John Hayward for revising my manuscript and for his unfailing help. I also wish to thank M Raymond Las Vergnas for his guidance.

Acknowledgments are due to Messrs Heinemann for permission to quote from Graham Greene's novels; to MM Julliard for permission to quote from M Rostenne's *Graham Greene Témoin des Temps Tragiques*; and to Les Editions du Seuil for permission to quote from *Dieu Vivant*.

CONTENTS

"I tell you, life would be unendurable
If you were wide awake . . ."
T. S. *Eliot*—THE FAMILY REUNION

"That face said as clearly as words that ideas never
changed, the world never moved; it lay there always,
the ravaged and disputed territory between the two
eternities."
Graham Greene—BRIGHTON ROCK

"Quand l'univers pèse tout entier sur nous, il n'y a
pas d'autre contrepoids possible que Dieu lui-même
. . . Le mal est infini au sens de l'indéterminé:
matière, espace, temps. Sur ce genre d'infini, seul le
véritable infini l'emporte. C'est pourquoi la croix est
une balance où un corps frêle et léger, mais qui
était Dieu, a soulevé le poids du monde entier.
'Donne-moi un point d'appui et je soulèverai le
monde.' Ce point d'appui est la croix. Il ne peut y
en avoir d'autre. Il faut qu'il soit à l'intersection du
monde et de ce qui n'est pas le monde. La croix est
cette intersection."
Simone Weil—LA PESANTEUR ET LA GRÂCE

INTRODUCTION

A BOY OF SEVENTEEN, still almost a child, but the leader of a "mob" of gangsters and several times a murderer, is driven to death in the cheap setting of Brighton; a "whisky-priest", a sinful coward, dies as a martyr in a "godless state" of Mexico; a successful police officer commits suicide in a damp, hot port on the West African coast: news items for the daily paper, the usual material of Graham Greene's waste land. But here a new light, which pierced only dimly through his first novels and 'entertainments', is turned on. Pinkie and the whisky-priest and Scobie, the leading characters around whose destiny the pattern of *Brighton Rock*, *The Power and the Glory* and *The Heart of the Matter* develops, are openly concerned with the issue of Salvation and Damnation. They are Catholics and they "know"; they are aware that a great conflict is raging and stand in the front line of the battlefield, in "the ravaged and disputed territory between the two eternities". They have lost too the innocence and irresponsibility of ignorance, and in a fallen world their minds are a prey to all the supernatural forces involved in the struggle. Like Harry in T. S. Eliot's play, *The Family Reunion*, they are wide awake to the nightmare. They are sinners, but tormented by the knowledge of their misery; because they believe, they measure their offence and know they belong to the race of the (apparently) damned.

This spiritual intensity, this quality of deep reality, is

1

the main unifying factor in these three consecutive novels and entitles us to treat them as a trilogy. They pose the problem of man's destiny, and, however different Pinkie and the whisky-priest and Scobie may be, they are all actors in the same tragedy, all endowed with the same essential longing for peace: " . . . dona nobis pacem". They can also be identified in many respects with Greene himself as a study of his travel-books reveals. Greene, we feel, has translated his own experience, his sharp and early sense of evil, in terms of fiction. He has lent to Pinkie some of his own memories of misery and of the cruelty of childhood. *The Power and the Glory* can best be studied in the light of *The Lawless Roads*, where the author himself indicates the sources of the novel; in the same way *The Heart of the Matter* was inspired by a trip to Liberia, reported in *Journey without Maps*, and a longer stay during the last war in Freetown, Sierra Leone. The issue of suicide, the "unforgivable sin", can similarly be traced back to Greene's adolescence and the personal experience revealed in 'The Revolver in a Corner Cupboard' (one of the essays collected in *The Lost Childhood*) and in 'The Gamble' (one of the early poems collected in *Babbling April*). This closeness to life and to our own world undoubtedly accounts for the sense of reality and truth deeply felt in these novels.

But, if these three novels stand apart in Greene's work as a unit, they are as closely related to it as they are to his direct experiences. In fact they only indicate a new stage in the development of the author's vision. All "Greeneland", as it has been called, is to be found here—the same obsessions or themes: pursuit, betrayal, escape, child-

2

hood, fear; the same shabby human material and the single pattern which gives the clue to the artist's creation. This "ruling fantasy which drove him to write" gives a remarkable continuity to his work and any part of it can be best explained by continuous reference to all the others. In an essay entitled 'The Lost Childhood', we are told that the reading of *The Viper of Milan*, by Marjorie Bowen, was for him the occasion when "the future for better or worse really struck". The story of Mastino della Scala, Duke of Verona, "who at last turned from an honesty that never paid and betrayed his friends and died dishonoured and a failure even at treachery", and of Gian Galeazzo Visconti, Duke of Milan, "with his beauty, his patience and his genius for evil", helped the young Greene to explain the world around him. Miss Bowen "had given me my pattern—religion might later explain it to me in other terms, but the pattern was already there —perfect evil walking the world where perfect good can never walk again, and only the pendulum ensures that after all in the end justice is done". This world where the ancient Nemesis, or fate, seems to rule, where man is imprisoned in a given 'situation', appears to be nonsensical. The misery of a Coral Musker or a Dr Czinner (*Stamboul Train*), of an Anthony Farrant (*England Made Me*) or a Raven (*A Gun for Sale*), seems hopeless. Greene shares the terror and anxiety of Camus and Kafka and of most modern writers when they face the condition of man. He is moved to compassion for all the displaced and the exiled of the world, for "the most shabby, the most corrupt, of his human actors", as much as Henry James to whom this statement is applied; he considers that

3

disloyalty is a virtue which enables him to feel "sympathy and a measure of understanding for those who lie outside the boundaries of State sympathy".

There is a close kinship between the characters of the trilogy and the whole Greenian family, but here we become aware that their particular acts, like those of Mauriac's characters, are less important than the force, whether God or Devil, that compels them. A "hint of an explanation" of such an odd world is suggested. "The devil—and God too—", Arthur Rowe thinks in *The Ministry of Fear*, "have always used comic people, little suburban natures and the maimed and warped to serve his purposes. When God used them you talked emptily of Nobility and when the devil used them of Wickedness, but the material was only dull shabby human mediocrity in either case." A significance is given to sin, suffering and the pain and misery of man. That is the mystery, indeed, "to reconcile that with the love of God".

The problem of determinism as against freedom in human destiny already underlay the first novels and 'entertainments' and gave a strange and unknown dimension to the ordinary thriller. But thenceforward, in his novels, "the artist's interest moved from sociology to eschatology", as Evelyn Waugh observed of *The Heart of the Matter*. Greene has reached maturity and with it the rank of a great writer. After denouncing the maladjustments of our social order in *It's a Battlefield* and international capitalism in *England made Me* in plain human terms, he was to approach the deepest mystery, for faith does not simplify. Following the line set by Pascal, Newman, Kierkegaard, he feels every day the

4

pain caused in body and spirit by the paradoxes of Christianity. Like them and with Simone Weil, he believes in the universality and inevitability of suffering and sin, in a world that weighs so heavily upon us that only the grace of God can lift the load. No one can "conceive . . . the appalling strangeness of the mercy of God", who died for all of us on the Cross—"the point of intersection of the timeless with time".

Pinkie and the whisky-priest and Scobie, set apart and isolated in the world surrounding them, are involved in the drama of freedom. In these three novels, through the medium of leading images, of tragic, concrete terms, Greene expresses his philosophy or rather his vision of life. He himself confesses, in a prefatory letter to Paul Rostenne's *Graham Greene Témoin des Temps Tragiques*, that it would embarrass him to discuss the ideas underlying his books, for he was driven by the destiny of his characters, while writing, and not by the desire to express his thoughts about the problems facing man. His books are not meant to be edifying but to give a picture of human nature. Here he appears to be close to Gabriel Marcel's notion of a Christian existentialism. It will be our purpose to try to understand these imaginary characters as men. We shall attempt to define their situation in the world and in time, the principles according to which they act, the structure of their minds, all the conditions that determine them to such an extent that some have doubted whether free will was still conceivable in their case and whether fate was not the only answer to their progress through life. At the end of the journey in the dark, "without maps", in the complete human failure, in

5

the huge abandonment of the desert, we shall hear a voice, our eyes will begin to see a dim reflection of the invisible light and to make out the mysterious pattern wrought by the Grace of a Living God, to whom the smallest act of faith or love is infinitely precious, working for the salvation of the least worthy of us.

PART ONE

"THE LANDSCAPE OF THE DRAMA"

★

" 'Why, this is Hell, nor are we out of it' . . . His
wife, the Empire burgundy, the empty files and the
vibration of locomotives on the line, they were the
important landscape of his great drama."
BRIGHTON ROCK

SEEDINESS, A SIGN of the maladjustments and injustice of
society, appeals very deeply to Greene's heart: "Even the
seediness of civilization, of the sky-signs in Leicester
Square, the 'tarts' in Bond Street, the smell of cooking
greens off Tottenham Court Road, the motor salesmen in
Great Portland Street." There one cannot help knowing
the worst, there nobody could "ever talk of a heaven on
earth", or forget the "terrible aboriginal calamity" which
pierced the heart of Newman and the misery of man
which filled Pascal with awe. This awareness of the worst,
of the underside of all things that seem good or beautiful,
of sin, of poverty, brings us to the drab quarters of the
big cities with the smell, the dirt and the smoke from the
steel factory buildings, the streets where torn pieces of
waste paper are whirled by the wind, the queues for cheap
seats at cinemas, the fish-and-chip shops, the "wilderness
of trams and second-hand clothes shops and public lava-
tories and evening institutes", to the gaudy shore of
Brighton, Tabasco "the godless state", the hot coast of
Sierra Leone. This is what man has "made out of the
primitive, what he has made out of childhood", the
world where murderers are born, where fathers are sent to
prison or mothers cut their throats with a carving knife,
and where a child—Raven in *A Gun for Sale*—is afflicted
with a harelip that conditions his misery; where a girl—
Else in *The Confidential Agent*—meets corruption too
early around her and is finally killed by a mad woman.

9

This is where Judas is born, the "Shape of Africa", the image recurrently used by Greene to visualize the misery of the world.

"To me Africa has always seemed an important image . . . 'You dreamed you were in Africa. Of what do you think first when I say the word Africa, Africa?' and a crowd of words and images, witches and death, unhappiness and the Gare St Lazare, the huge smoky viaduct over a Paris slum, crowd together and block the way to full consciousness." This confession of Greene's in *Journey without Maps* explains the unconscious principle at work when he chooses the setting of his dramas. There is a "quality of darkness" or "a sense of despair needed". The strength of this image of Africa, "not a particular place, but a shape, a strangeness, a wanting to know", is further accounted for in 'The Lost Childhood'. We know how important, in the author's eyes, the impressions of childhood are; it is a recurrent theme in his work, and is probably related to the psychoanalytic treatment to which he was submitted in adolescence when he was given to suicidal fantasies. We are told in this essay that *King Solomon's Mines* by Rider Haggard certainly influenced his future. The land of the Kukuanas and Liberia, as well as the other dark places of the world, "belonged to the same continent and, however distantly, to the same region of the imagination—the region of uncertainty, of not knowing the way about". Conrad's *Heart of Darkness*, one of the books Greene greatly admires, is also another image of the same vision. The experience of Kurtz seen through Marlow's eyes shows that savagery, the mysterious life of the wilderness, "has a fascination . . . the

10

fascination of the abomination". This man who was taken by the way of solitude, of silence, to primaeval regions was there assaulted by powers of darkness and died tormented in his agony by a terrible vision, "the horror, the horror", hell.

For Greene, the theme of departure, of the journey to the heart of darkness, whether it be Africa, Mexico or even the human heart, corresponds to a "sense of nostalgia for something lost", to a desire "to recall at which point we went astray", to an attempt to find something hidden by too much cerebration, "one's place in time, based on a knowledge not only of one's present but of the past from which one has emerged". The presence of evil is the first thing we apprehend. Beauty is too often a deceiving trick of the devil, tempting us by the appearances of what we only desire for ourselves, charming our intelligence or our senses. We must not forget that Satan was the most beautiful among the angels. The whisky-priest exclaims: "I know from experience how much beauty Satan carried down with him when he fell. Nobody ever said the fallen angels were the ugly ones. Oh no, they were just as quick and light and . . ." And in *The Third Man*: "Evil was like Peter Pan—it carried with it the horrifying and horrible gift of eternal youth." The beauty of Dorian Gray has a horrifying and dark counterpart. And this is why Greene very seldom indulges in images of beauty and prefers to turn to the drab and the seedy rather than to "the smart, the new, the chic, the cerebral": to come closer to the beginning, to point out the maladjustments rather than the great achievements in which men put their trust and for which

11

they make gods of themselves, and forget the only true reality.

The shape of Africa, the heart of darkness, corresponds also to a state of lawlessness in a no-man's-land on a restless border; a solidarity exists between all the lawless of the world, and again memories of childhood are evoked to help to explain the recurrence of the theme. Even as a child at Berkhamsted, Greene could detect around him the "genuine quality of evil. . . . In the land of the skyscrapers, of stone stairs and cracked bells ringing early, one was aware of fear and hate, a kind of lawlessness." The misery of the world spreads out in circles like Dante's hell. "This is only the outer circle", says the Police Commissioner in *It's a Battlefield* after visiting Drover in his cell. "Why, this is Hell, nor are we out of it." It's Mr Prewitt, Pinkie's ridiculous lawyer, who produces the answer of Mephistopheles to Faustus when he asked where Hell was. There is no escape from it, it is "walled in with steel". As Pinkie cannot escape from Brighton, so the whisky-priest is called back to the Godless State and Scobie, isolated by the war, cannot leave the "Coast". "There is no peace anywhere where there is human life, but there are, I told myself, quiet and active sectors of the line. . . . The horror may be the same, it is an intrinsic part of human life in every place: it attacks you in the Strand or the Tropics; but where the eagles are gathered together, it is not unnatural to expect to find the Son of Man as well." (*The Lawless Roads.*) There it is not possible, for one who sees and knows, to live in an ugly indifference. Greene exclaims during the bombarding of London in the last war: "The world we lived in could not

12

have ended any other way. The curious waste lands one sometimes saw from trains . . . the dingy fortune-teller's on the first floor above the cheap permanent waves in a Brighton back street; they all demanded violence . . . an old dog-toothed civilization is breaking now." The world is the prison where we are held captive. War is the inevitable end called for by this corruption, and while it has not reached yet the gaudy shore of Brighton, it has left wounds still bleeding in the Mexico of *The Power and the Glory* and it is actually raging in *The Heart of the Matter*. But only through violence and hell are we brought to Faith and Heaven. When the enemy is disclosed, one is not so easily deceived.

These qualities of shabbiness, darkness, lawlessness, are common to the world which Greene's characters inhabit. But each of them possesses a single and unique environment which contributes to the definition of his personality, which colours his existence in an original way. Our position in the world, in society, enforces limitations upon us. We are isolated in our own personal world and can never penetrate fully into the 'territories' of others, even when we love. But our relations with men are also part of our 'belongings'. We must bear this in mind while we examine the world of Pinkie and the whisky-priest and Scobie.

II "THE POPULOUS FORESHORE
OF BRIGHTON"

BRIGHTON IS PINKIE'S territory. He is a "local"; everywhere else he would be a stranger. But it is also the world

13

of Ida Arnold, who is nowhere a stranger; the same place on the English coast and yet so different according to the point of view taken. As always, with Greene, we are presented with multiple aspects of the same position in place or time. Described through the direct impressions of some character, it takes on a spiritual significance corresponding to the intensity of reality presented by the viewer himself. Here, we are taken mainly through three "shapes" of Brighton: Ida's and Colleoni's bright and lustful world, the dark world inherited by Pinkie from Kite as from an adoptive father, and Nelson Place, his home, his past which he shares with Rose. Between Ida's and Pinkie's territories there is only a physical likeness; Greene insists repeatedly on their complete strangeness to each other. The boy will try to escape, to add all the visible world possessed by Colleoni to his own, but in vain; he is relentlessly called back to Nelson Place, not even keeping Kite's inheritance, because his own interior law is irremediably different and involves these foreign territories in a defensive struggle. There probably lies the real explanation of Ida's and Colleoni's war against Pinkie: a natural revolt against invasion.

The tripper's eye sees, when Brighton is at its best, with the Bank holiday crowds or at the races, only bright sunshine on an ignorant world and the gaudy setting of a popular summer resort; a cosmopolitan scene where people of all sorts come down for week-ends to make love in hotel bedrooms and to enjoy the fun, walking on the Front, entering the Palace of Pleasure, with shooting booths, band-stands and miniature cars tear-

14

ing round the curve, looking at the sea "stretched like a piece of gay common washing on a tenement square across the end of a street", the colour of Ida's eyes.

"It's homely . . . it's what I like," Ida thinks; her laughter is reassuring and her huge friendly bosom is offered as a hiding-place from all pain and misery. She is life triumphant, a blind force of nature, brooking no resistance, a "monstrous Cybele", as Jacques Madaule puts it in his study of Greene's work. She has all the carnality and sensual warmth of the body, and endless vitality. "Life was sunlight on brass bedposts, ruby port, the leap of the heart when the outsider you have backed passes the post, and the colours go bobbing up. Life was poor Fred's mouth pressed down on hers in the taxi, vibrating with the engine along the parade." There is no harm in her but a determined sense of justice on earth, "an eye for an eye". She believes in life and in right and wrong, not in Heaven and Hell, nor in death which is to her the end of everything. Her mind works with "the simplicity and the regularity of a sky-sign". She belongs to "the great middle law-abiding class".

Ida exemplifies the only simple solution—the absence of faith. She is reduced almost to a symbol, a kind of mythological embodiment of an idea rather than a living character. She has the same superficiality as the Brighton she knows. She sees nothing of the deep secret truth, she is completely unaware of "the darkness in which the boy walked, going from Frank's, going back to Frank's". She will never be a mature, responsible person; she belongs like Sylvie, Spicer's girl, to everybody yet to nobody. She becomes the instrument of fate, the Erinys defending

15

her faith in life, avenging the death of Hale, pursuing Pinkie because he does not fit in her world. In this world of nature, we remember Lucy in *The Man Within*, endowed with the same carnality and ignorance of the dark, or Mabel in *Stamboul Train*, fighting to subdue Dr Czinner. In *Brighton Rock* we find Colleoni, who possesses the visible world, living with his gold lighter in his elegant suite in the luxury of the Cosmopolitan, from which Pinkie and Rose will be rejected.

In "Kite's territory" a new light has been turned on. The sea washes "round the piles at the end of the pier, dark poison-green". We still walk along the Palace Pier, penetrate into Snow's or Sherry's, but the atmosphere is different. We are with the lawless. Hale knew that "this was real now: the boy, the razor cut, life going out with the blood in pain". Murder waits for him under "the little covered arcade where the cheap shops stood between the sea and the stone wall, selling Brighton Rock". By contrast with Colleoni's big-business manners, which nourish the Boy's ambitions, the "mob" meets in his room at Frank's, sitting on the brass bedstead, dirty with the crumbs of sausage-rolls, with the shabby wash-stand and the money hidden in the soap-dish. This at least is where Pinkie thinks he belongs, where he feels at home, until a girl gets "mixed up" with him, alters everything, the order he had assigned to his belongings; by her very presence she drives him out of the security he had wrought for himself, and destroys his ambitions.

In this "place of accidents and unexplained events", Kite's gang is now under Pinkie's leadership, looking up

16

to him like children. Cubbitt, Dallow, Spicer, also are to
a certain extent innocent; they mean no real harm; a bit
of "carving" from time to time is the rule of the game;
but they don't stand for murder. At their own level they
are just ordinary men, afraid of pain and death and given
to the usual passions of grown-up people. Spicer, a
middle-aged grey-haired man, dreams of a holiday and
retirement: "A pal of mine keeps the 'Blue Anchor' in
Union Street. A Free-House. High class. Lunches served.
He's often said to me, 'Spicer, why don't you come into
partnership? We'd make the old place into a hotel with
a few more nickers in the till.' " He has a girl too, and is a
sentimental chap attached to people he has lived with.
But he is scared and dangerous, and for that reason will
die. Cubbitt in a moment of revolt and drunkenness will
betray the boy to Ida and run away. Dallow, "a stout
muscular man with a broken nose and an expression of
brutal simplicity", lusting after Frank's wife, Judy, will
be Pinkie's faithful follower and friend, sharing his dark
secrets, giving him advice, defending him against his
crazy, dangerous impulses. Also involved with the gang
is Prewitt, the lawyer, whose miserable existence is
revealed in his Sunday drunkenness. Yet all of them,
however closely tied up with Pinkie's destiny they may
be, do not share his mad purpose, his knowledge of yet
another darker world.

As for Kite, whose world all this really is, whose death
has started the long chain of murders, we shall never
know exactly who he was apart from his importance in
Pinkie's life, comparable to Carlyon's for Andrews in *The
Man Within*. He had picked him up on the Palace Pier,

17

perhaps because "he needed a little sentiment". He had been killed, but the boy had prolonged his existence, "not touching liquor, biting his nails in the Kite way", taking his place in the large room used as headquarters for the mob. "It had been as if a father had died, leaving him an inheritance it was his duty never to leave for strange acres." But there is another inheritance which he wishes in vain to forget.

Nelson Place is the last circle of hell, concealed by false superficial appearances. Going further to find "the shabby secret behind the bright corsage" and a territory of extreme poverty, we come to the common world of Pinkie and Rose—his own past making claims, though he thought he had escaped from it for ever. But one never escapes from one's past and he has to make an unwilling and bitter pilgrimage to "that drab dynamited plot of ground they both called home", where children play among the rubble. His own house is gone now; the room at the bend of the stairs where "the Saturday Night exercise" has taken place is just air. But he can look at the exact duplicate of it when he goes through the awful little passage which "stinks like a lavatory" to ask Rose's parents to let her marry him. She brings him back his own past; she is Nelson Place, with her thin pale face of sixteen, having known no other luxury than a twopenny ice from an Everest tricycle. When she finds Kolley Kibber's card under the table-cloth in Snow's, she is just new there, just out of the hole where are "murder, copulation, extreme poverty, fidelity and the love and fear of God", and which Pinkie had left years ago through

18

revolt; but she has not the strength for that nor the ambition, and she is good. She is pitiable, like Coral Musker in *Stamboul Train* but, like her, capable of responsibility, of devotion to someone with whom she intuitively finds something in common. She shares with Pinkie "youth and shabbiness and a kind of ignorance in the dapper café" and above all faith. They are both "Romans", like Piker, the young waiter in the road-house whom Pinkie will cruelly mock. Rose feels at once her link with Pinkie, and does not hesitate to get "mixed up". In her simplicity, she gives herself to him, promises an entire fidelity, without calculating the cost, ready to love him whatever it may mean. He cannot help feeling she completes him. She, through her contact with him, will mature, learning in her love something new—not only the escape from the past or the expectations of the future, but the fullness of the intense moments of life, love, death, motherhood too, and the pain accompanying them. We shall see how deeply she works, without knowing it, in Pinkie's mind and soul, facing with him and for him Ida's determined will in an opposition recalling that of Elizabeth and Lucy in *The Man Within*, between the carnal prostitute and the good woman fulfilling an invisible spiritual mission.

III   TABASCO, "THE GODLESS STATE"

The Power and the Glory is, of all Greene's novels, the most directly inspired by his actual experience, as recorded in *The Lawless Roads*. The imagination of the

19

novelist has worked within limits clearly defined by the historical data gathered during a trip to Mexico in the spring of 1938, when he was commissioned to write a book on the religious situation. Not content with investigating it in comparative comfort and security, he felt called to the centre of something; as in Liberia, he was ready to suffer the difficulties and inconveniences of a hard journey on a dingy boat, or by mule, through a desolate wilderness, a land of heat, vultures and swamps, to find the primitiveness, not of man, but of Faith and Evil in an officially godless state. It is not the first time that Greene has touched on the subject of the violent, dark approach to a faith mingled with superstition, so strange to an Englishman controlled by so much puritan reserve. In *Rumour at Nightfall*, Chase complains of the effects the "strange standards" and "dark atmosphere" of the Spanish faith have on him.

Here we meet with another typical example of Greene's method of symbolization. Mexico, like Africa, becomes another image; it is a state of mind, violence and faith and life "under the shadow of religion—of God or the Devil"—against anarchy. As Paul Rostenne writes, "the particular value of Greene's work lies in his throwing light on the ontological character of contemporary violence, long before its latest and most conspicuous outbursts. 'Perhaps we are in need of violence'." In Mexico Greene was reminded of the "aboriginal calamity" perceived by Newman, for violence in our world conveys a religious meaning. It is brought up as a reaction against a totalitarian government, interfering with all human activities, giving them a collective orientation. Greene

20

denounces the idol, the State, which does not think in terms of human beings and is led to persecute any enemy for the common good. "Perhaps the only body in the world to-day which consistently—and sometimes success-fully—opposes the totalitarian State is the Catholic Church", because it has always had for its mission the destruction of all our idols. Mexico is but an image of the Dark Ages which seem to have come again and in which we are brought back to a true religion, purified from any complacent compromise with the world—the world which appears at last as it is: a prison.

The impression made upon Greene by his journey was so strong that he set about writing one of his greatest and most significant books. *The Power and the Glory* was pub-lished in 1940, just after *The Lawless Roads*. It is as though a kind of necessity drove him on, as if he were possessed by the character and the soul of the nameless priest "who existed for ten years in the forests and swamps". Terms and images used in the travel-book are directly transferred to the novel. These two books pro-vide a unique example of the nature and the real purpose of Greene's art and of the mechanism of his creative mind. His only addition to reality in the novel lies in the characterization of his human material, in the power to conjure up life and the interior history of a man. The entire background is as close to actual fact as possible.

Twice in the book we catch a glimpse of the (compara-tively) free and sinless world on the other side of the border. It seems to be introduced solely to emphasize the horror and the abandonment as well as the greater reality of

21

the "walled in" world, from which there are only two
ways of escape. The hunted priest tries them both; when
the story opens, he has come down to the port, in one of
his periodical attempts to take the boat for "the forty-
two hours in the Gulf to Vera-Cruz". But for the last
time he is driven back to the darkness inland, the heat,
the heavy air, while on the *General Obregon* a faint
breeze begins to blow. "There was an enormous sense of
freedom and air upon the Gulf with the low tropical
shore-line buried in darkness as deeply as any mummy in
a tomb. I am happy, the young girl said to herself without considering why, I am happy"—as though a terrible
load had been suddenly removed.

The same impression is conveyed later on, when, after
a long exhausting journey across the mountains and a
bare plateau, the priest falls asleep by the wall of a
church with the cheerful peal of bells as an accompani-
ment of his dreams. There we catch sight of paradise, as
Greene himself did near Palenque at the bungalow of the
German, Herr R., a Lutheran, who had actually shel-
tered a priest. The Lehrs of *The Power and the Glory* are
the exact replicas of this man and his sister. In their
world are peace and tranquillity, and cleanliness. Like
Ida Arnold, however different they are from her, they
recognize a law of right and wrong; not for them the
"prying insight of fellow Catholics", always able to detect
the presence of evil. Miss Lehr had once had her eyes
opened by the *Police News*, but had decided that it was
better left aside and ignored. "Mr Lehr and his sister had
combined to drive out savagery by simply ignoring anything that conflicted with an ordinary German-American

22

homestead. It was, in its way, an admirable mode of life."

The pious, complacent people—the man in the cantina who used to be Treasurer to the Guild of the Blessed Sacrament, the people in Las Casas, all those bound by the habit of piety—also belong to this world. The priest's past belongs to it too—the rich parish churches, the confessions, the holy images and bargaining for the price of baptism. But this reminder of the past, the movements of Miss Lehr, as she wraps up the sandwiches, have no more reality than the priest's dreams, and when the other world, in the person of the half-caste, stretches a hand across the border, he feels just as if he were awaking from another dream, like Hale in Brighton when he sees Pinkie.

In the huge abandonment of Tabasco no churches remain standing; no stream for bathing, nothing left but the heat, the vultures looking for carrion, the swamps and the puritan shabby capital (the Villa-Hermosa described in *The Lawless Roads* and in the short story, 'The Lottery Ticket') where all lights are out by nine-thirty, and alcohol is prohibited. Everywhere the same cry rises out of solitude and decay: "We have been deserted." An immense sadness overwhelms the heart, with a sense of universal death. Greene himself had felt "that this wasn't a country to live in at all with the heat and the desolation; it was a country to die in and leave only ruins behind". Destruction has passed over the world; man has challenged God, who has left him in an unbearable solitude. In this evil land, "the only place

23

where you can find some symbol of your faith is in the cemetery up on a hill above the town", where you get the sense of a "far better and cleaner city than that of the living at the bottom of the hill". This is the world made by the Lieutenant of Police, but his task of destruction will never be completed, because faith is still present and wages ceaseless war against him.

On the fringe of the conflict, not knowing that they are involved in it, Dr Tench, the dentist, and the Fellows stand like children lost in a strange world. The unhappy married couple in the banana-station are in many respects close to the Scobies, without the complexity of the latter's Catholicism. Strangers in the land they live in (though Captain Fellows feels attached to it) and strangers to their child, who is out of place with them because they live on memories from another world she does not know, they eventually fly from the wild land that has taken her from them. Dr Tench, an exiled Englishman, annihilated by the climate and by the hopeless and awful conditions of life, was inspired by the American Doc. Winter, met by Greene wandering "without a memory and without a hope in the immense heat". By the nature of his profession (a flourishing one in Mexico), he is associated with pain, and has a human understanding of the small man of disreputable appearance to whom he displays his belongings; it is through his eyes and through his feelings of nausea and desertion that we watch the death of the priest. He is merely another victim of fate, which in his case struck in a waste-paper basket.

In the poor villages of Tabasco, faith is anchored deep

in the hearts of the suffering people of God. The forbidden Mass, heard in secret, recalls the scenes of the Roman catacombs. These peons have no instruction, but they have sucked Faith with the milk at their mothers' breasts. They squeeze "one more mortification out of their harsh and painful lives". They are the same people who commit all the ordinary human sins and crimes and go to prison for them. But they die as hostages rather than betray the priest. There is also the extraordinary faith of the Indian woman bearing her dead child to the grove of crosses on the plateau, rising "like a short-cut to the dark, magical heart of faith". These people know the sign that marks the priest with a dignity no sin can delete. Judas, the half-caste, knows it too, the evil heart at which "salvation could strike like lightning"; and so does the pitiable married priest, weak and humble in the knowledge of his immense sin, who is opposed to the whisky-priest and with him represents what is left of the Church. As the man in the Academia Commercial explains to his wife: "The Church is Padre José and the whisky-priest."

The Lieutenant of Police is the whisky-priest's direct opponent, as Ida is Pinkie's. There is, however, a great difference here: God's enemy is no longer a simple force of nature; he symbolizes the modern Prometheus. He is a Christian who has revolted but cannot return to a purely natural condition, for "there is no other solution for Christian people or nations who break away from Christianity but to become antichristian". Even if he denies that there is a God, and like Nietzsche exclaims triumphantly "God is dead", the very intensity of his

25

hate can only be the effect of a belief still alive in spite of his own will. "Can you hate something you don't believe in?" And yet Blacker in 'The Hint of an Explanation' called himself a free-thinker. "What an impossible paradox, to be free and to be so obsessed." A substitute for God has to be found, when God is deserted. "It seems necessary", Paul Rostenne writes, "if modern atheism is to exist at all, that it should appear in a religious guise and mobilize for its own purpose feelings and aspirations which are specifically supernatural. Hence the profoundly religious temperament and ardent craving for the absolute of the most aggressive atheists. One must need God terribly badly to give oneself up body and soul to one of his substitutes, whether a man or an idea."

The Lieutenant, in revolt against the Church he had seen at work in his childhood oppressing the poor, in revolt against the pain and the misery of the peons, is now entirely devoted to a new cult. He wants to create happiness for his people, to give them the whole world, the truth about this vacant universe and cooling world, "to begin the world again with them in the desert", and this by any means, even a massacre. He is actuated by a terrible passion for power, assuming for himself the creative action of God, destroying what he has made, ready to eradicate from the world all marks of God in a gigantic and desperate attempt, for man would have to destroy himself in order to kill God.

The religious intensity of his passion is stressed repeatedly: "There was something of a priest in his intent observant walk", in his ascetic life, ironically con-

26

trasted with the corruption of the whisky-priest. He is also moved to a genuine compassion for the poor and unhappy, as is shown with a particular significance when *YES* he gives unknowingly the price of a Mass to the whisky-priest. He is touched by the humility and understanding of his victim when he faces him in a last fight in which each defends his position, the one religious, the other profane, but in which both are at one in the intensity of their belief and their immense craving for justice. In many ways the Lieutenant resembles Pinkie: the same revolt against the world of childhood; the same ascetic life and shrinking from the sexual act; the same pride, though in the Lieutenant hate is unconsciously directed entirely at God, while a sense of responsibility drives him to feel sympathy for his fellow men.

Children and adolescents always appeal to Greene's heart, and above all those who too early have to face the awful and terrible reality of life and suffering. In the dark state of Mexico, they mature too young; the load is too heavy for their thin bodies. Such children constantly come between the Lieutenant of Police and the whisky-priest and play an important part in the development of the action. Brigitta with her old-young face, whose corruption is the priest's atonement for his sin, leads him to a pure selfless love; Coral, independent, inflexible, prepared, waits for her cue to a mysterious knowledge and a violent death. Her father is aware of her resemblance to the Lieutenant of Police; she belongs to the world which he has created and which has imparted to her a wildness confusing to her parents; like him she is conscious of heavy responsibilities and is able to detect a sign of

27

greatness in the whisky-priest. She has the intent mind and passionate nature, which are the materials from which saints are made. While her body comes to maturity, her heart, controlled by a simple acceptance of men and things, is an empty room ready to receive God.

Children with bellies swollen from eating earth and by worms; the small boy with brown eyes waiting with infinite patience for the priest to come to his dying mother; the boy repelled by the pious story read to him by his mother, but welcoming the new priest at the end of the book; the dead child buried like a dog, without a prayer, and the baby killed by the gringo; they are all innocents caught in the great turmoil and expressing the tragedy of the land they live in, "waiting through the dry months and the rains for the footstep, the voice, 'Is it easier to say your sins be forgiven you . . .?' "

IV   THE "COAST"

THE SETTING OF *The Heart of the Matter*, like that of *The Power and the Glory*, is based on personal experience originally recorded in a travel-book; but in this case there is a twelve years' lag between the publication of *Journey Without Maps* in 1936 and the novel in 1948, and in the interval Greene had spent a year in Freetown during 1942 and 1943. It is to this visit that the story of Scobie can be traced back. Greene had made several unsuccessful attempts in 1936 to turn his African experience into fiction. In *The Heart of the Matter* he seems at last to have succeeded in delivering himself of the long-contemplated theme of Africa, and more specifically the "Coast", that rim of land "not so far from the central darkness". The geographical and historical background of the novel is derived from the author's contact with "the squalor and the unhappiness and the involuntary injustices of tired men", and from the experience of inertia gained there, where "worms and malaria, even without yellow fever, are enough to cloud life". The scene is like Brighton "parasitic, cosmopolitan, corrupt", in Evelyn Waugh's words, and the climate similar to Tabasco's.

There is little genuine primitiveness in the cosmopolitan world of the ruled. The natives have been spoilt by the seedy civilization introduced by the British. They are creoles and not "real niggers" as in the Protectorate. They try to imitate the civilization of white men, who are afraid of them. It is with this corrupt people that Scobie has to deal. He has to pronounce judgments when there is no evidence of absolute guilt or innocence. These men can never be fully understood; they still belong to their ancestral world, capable of patience when necessary, inevitably more at one with the land they live in than the British are. One begins in time to understand them and to grow fond of these people who paralyse an alien form of justice by so simple a method as telling lies; one becomes aware of the beauty of the young black girls and of the gorgeous sunsets "when all the laterite paths [turn] suddenly for a few minutes the colour of a rose"— one of Greene's very rare and fugitive images of beauty, which recurs in the novel and the travel-book as well and haunts the memory long after the actual experience.

29

The boys are always "all right". They are "real niggers". They appear throughout the novel as the members of a huge family, all brothers or half-brothers, establishing a secret liaison between their British masters. Ali, Scobie's boy for fifteen years, is more than a servant, is a faithful companion, making the camp-bed by the roadside, boiling tea in the police van on the "trek" through the forest to the dark interior, bandaging the bruised hand. Ali is for Scobie a symbol of security, solitude, happiness. Greene himself had felt the same deep affection for his own boy, Amedoo, the best in Freetown.

While the natives form the background of the story, the Syrians in the diamond business provide, ironically enough, a kind of projection of the war into this colony far from the actual front line. The rivalry between the Catholic Tallitt and the Mohammedan Yusef is further reflected in the underground conflict between the Europeans supporting them, which is one form of the antagonism between Wilson and Scobie. Yusef is, as genuinely as a Yusef can be, really moved, despite his corrupted nature, by a kind of admiration for the Just. His devotion and interest take the form of a satanic influence gradually driving Scobie further down. He impersonates the dark side of Scobie, as Scobie admits in his own words and with appropriate imagery when, during an important scene at Yusef's, he speaks of "the dark furnishings of hell". In Yusef's victory, there is an evil joy at having blackened goodness and integrity, and also disappointment at not having found after all the absolute goodness and justice unconsciously demanded by the blackest heart.

*　　　*　　　*

The British have brought their civilization to this colony, a home from home. "This was an English capital city; England had planted this town, the tin shacks and the Remembrance Day posters, and had then withdrawn up the hillside to smart bungalows, with wide windows and electric fans and perfect service." (*Journey Without Maps.*) The headquarters of the Empire have sent to the outposts men who were given "a feeling of respectability and a sense of fairness withering in the heat". The impression gathered by a tourist passing through Freetown before the war was one of complete lack of adaptation to the natives' world. The apparent order is but a rhetorical conception. The law defended by Scobie is fake, "with no connection with morals or justice". The grandiloquent boast of the police station is only one room deep: it conceals the odour of human meanness and injustice. People rot, like books; their age here is told by their years of service. "It's a climate for meanness, malice, snobbery, but anything like hate or love drives a man off his head."

Such is the world in which Scobie had lived for fifteen years, first alone, then with a wife. He had known a time when one could look forward to employing four boys and to having regular leaves, but a war waged far away had changed the conditions of life. The black-out darkens the city in the evening; a piece of Argentine beef is an occasion to celebrate; ships sink at sea and it becomes difficult to get away.

Harris is simply a lost child, doomed from his early schooldays at Downham. We are reminded immediately of Greene's schooldays at Berkhamsted, described in *The*

31

Lawless Roads, and his criticism of the whole system in *The Old School*. Like Minty in *England Made Me*, Harris is one more victim of a childish fidelity to his Alma Mater, never developing into a full mature personality, trying to forget his hatred for this awful country and "the loyalty we all feel to unhappiness" in a comic cockroach championship.

Wilson's habit of deceit and lustfulness hidden under a shy romanticism will be fostered by a few weeks in the port. The smooth surface betrayed by brown dog's eyes will soon be wiped off, and his voice, sounding like English spoken in England, will soon alter. Entrusted with a secret spying mission on the British officials, falling in love with Scobie's wife ("literary Louise"), driven on by mounting jealousy, Wilson symbolizes the fallen unconscious world, and represents the theme of the hunt, though only as a secondary element in the drama. His introduction into the first two parts of the novel is designed as a diversion from the more tragic first and third parts; but it is through his eyes that we first see Scobie and he is present at the end as he was at the beginning.

Louise is a weak character, a neurotic unable to overcome her strong dissatisfaction and take her share of the load instead of making continuous demands on others, and especially on her husband. Shaken by the death of her only child, she feeds on memories, storing them up to fill an inner vacancy, on books and on poetry as an escape from bitter reality, wincing at the sight of blood, depending as women often do on pride, "pride in themselves, their husbands, their surroundings . . . seldom

32

proud of the invisible". She is a failure as a wife and as a woman, unattractive, disliked, alienating others by her patronizing attitude and her blunders, a pitiable creature unable to inspire love except in a Wilson. She has little personality but a veneer of conventions and habits; even her religion, the Catholicism she shares with her husband, is close to the complacent piety of the woman in the Mexican prison, for whom the priest felt there was nothing to be done. She has, however, moments of lucidity and intuition about her husband, herself, and their relationship; she creates scenes in which the truth at last is spoken and it appears that she knows more than she seems to. Jealousy, when she comes back from her trip to South Africa, and action to bring her husband back to her, seem to quicken in her a new spring of life, and to strengthen her personality, but it is only a self-centred revival; nothing can shake her smugness. She is another victim of the climate, slyly working away at the disintegration of people and things; and we do not know what deep causes move her, for we are given no more than hints of what is going on in her mind.

Coming from another world after forty days and nights at sea in an open boat, lying on stretchers, suffering children are ferried across the river at Pende into Scobie's world. They are the innocent victims of the great conflict. The child of six, who dies while Scobie tries to comfort her, is mysteriously linked with his own dead daughter, the "pious nine-year-old girl's face in the white muslin of first communion". With her a young woman "ugly with exhaustion", holding a stamp-album, lies unconscious. Helen Rolt is little more than a schoolgirl, for her short married life has left no mark; alone and purposeless in this strange port, she is afraid of "the awful responsibility of receiving sympathy", much as Coral Musker in *Stamboul Train* was afraid of life in an unfamiliar world. A mutual craving for security leads to her and Scobie becoming involved. She will learn how to grow old and cruel; she will take on the look of the Coast, like everybody else, and become more and more like Louise. But there is a great difference between her and Louise; she does not "know" and Scobie's problems as a Catholic remain strange to her, though at the end she seems deeply touched by his contact. According to Greene no one can get deeply mixed up with a Catholic without being affected by it.

The Nissen hut allocated to her with its government furniture, its bareness and lack of memories, looks very much like Scobie's room at the Police Station, which is much more his home than the house he shares with Louise, who has filled it with her own belongings.

V   FATE IN PURSUIT

SUCH IS THE overwhelming misery of the world surrounding Pinkie, the whisky-priest and Scobie. We have seen how its multi-storied structure is represented by corresponding differences between individuals, how various planes of reality encircle the dark centre, like the ripples on the surface of water extending further and further from the fall of a stone. The outer circle of (apparent) innocence is endowed with a much thinner reality. There, as in San Antonio, "the horror and the beauty of human life [are] both absent. It is a passing sensation, for the ivory tower has its own horror: [that] of exclusion." Ida Arnold is one of those intruders whose knowledge of life was, as Marlow in *Heart of Darkness* felt, an "irritating pretence", because he was so sure they could not possibly know the things he knew. Happiness can be found at that stage, but only as a kind of protection against an inner vacancy. This conviction is found already in Greene's early verse:

> "*I could have been happy had I kept*
> *A certain godly distance from the world* . . .
> *I felt the ecstasy, I knew the pain.*"

"Point me out the happy man", Scobie thinks, "and I will point you out either egotism, selfishness, evil—or else an absolute ignorance." Under the apparent peace, a burning fire smoulders. The closer one gets to the centre, the more aware one becomes of the wrenching pain; Pinkie or the Lieutenant will try to rebel against it, while the whisky-priest and Scobie catch a glimpse of the depths where "the heart of the matter" is concealed. "If one knew . . . the facts, would one have to feel pity even for the planets? If one reached what they called the heart of the matter?"

Such is the landscape of the drama, the setting provided for its protagonists in the world and among people —the elements of their destiny. Now, we are told, concerning Ida Arnold, that "man is made by the places in which he lives". This statement could be applied to most

35

of Greene's characters. Pinkie, the whisky-priest and Scobie are trapped in this closed world and suffocating atmosphere; they cannot break away from it in order to take an objective view of their environment. Their environment thus becomes of very great importance, and this is why the technique of the cine-camera eye, much favoured by modern novelists, is so appropriate to the realization of such characters. Unlike the heroes of classical tragedy, or at least to a much greater extent than they, Greene's characters need an 'aura' of images and sensations to give them reality, to compensate, as it were, for their failure in self-creation. Their personality is not sufficiently developed for them to rise above their 'situation' in the world.

Pinkie, the whisky-priest and Scobie are also the victims of time. Like the characters of Kafka's world they seem to have no control over unexplained events. They are led by fate to their end, "carried like children in a coach through the huge spaces without any knowledge of their destination". They give the impression of drifting with the flow of history. When they attempt to turn against it, they get drowned by higher waves. Greene's characters are generally destined to die violent deaths. To all of them the lines by Dryden, quoted as an epigraph to *The Power and the Glory*, are applicable:

> "*Th' inclosure narrow'd; the sagacious power*
> *Of hounds and death drew nearer every hour.*"

Claude-Edmonde Magny comments in her preface to the French translation of *Brighton Rock*: "Fate is a situation. It is indeed the human situation in the highest sense of the word, since man cannot dissociate himself from his individual predicament."

The technique of the thriller is quite proper for expressing this theme of pursuit. It is used in all Greene's books, with a more definite emphasis on the detective element in the 'entertainments', whereas in the novels we are discussing increasing importance is given to what appears to be the metaphysical significance of the drama. The plot takes us through a continuous, logical and closely linked chain of events to the last moment when the story winds up, with the human instrument chosen by destiny relentless in pursuit. Andrews in *The Man Within* wonders "whether he would ever know peace from pursuit"; Dr Czinner is the prey of Mabel Warrant in *Stamboul Train*; D., the Confidential Agent, in the novel of that name, knows no respite during his short stay in England.

Destiny seems to strike at any moment, which the victim has no means of foreseeing, and then there is no escape from it and no explanation. When the dramatic stories of Pinkie, the whisky-priest and Scobie open, we feel that the pendulum is about to swing. Heavy clouds seem to occlude the sky above their heads. And we are aware, as Greene was in *The Viper of Milan*, of the "sense of doom that lies over success".

This feeling is particularly strong in the case of Pinkie. The grey-eyed Boy, seventeen-year-old leader of Kite's gang, wields an extraordinary power over his middle-aged followers. All the brains of the "mob" are concentrated in him: " 'You take account of most things,' Dallow said with admiration." His cunning and cold-

37

blooded attention to every detail ensure his success; the police are blind to the truth, he controls life and death, his ambition is limitless. This is the moment chosen by destiny as the turning point; its instrument will be Ida, who undertakes to revenge Hale. She moves slowly but with unshaking purpose; nothing can resist her indomitable will. The Boy is more and more closely encircled until he feels his grip loosening and there is no escape left but suicide. His entanglement with Rose, necessary though involuntary, undermines his abnormal strength, Hale's murder, a revenge for Kite's, was the first in a chain of events: Rose seeing the card placed by Spicer under the table-cloth, Spicer's murder, Cubbitt's betrayal and finally Dallow's and Ida's interference with Pinkie's project, and Pinkie's suicide—all this within a few weeks; and yet, "if Kite had been there, he would never have got mixed up".

The small man, looking like a black question mark, with the "round and hollow face charred with a three-days' beard" who interrupts Dr Tench's thoughts turns out to be the last priest left in the State, where he has succeeded in living for ten years, going from village to village, saying Mass in secret: a whisky-priest, who has gradually surrendered all habits of piety and given way to the 'itch of the flesh' in a moment of despair and drunkenness, but for all this the only one in the whole State through whom God still exists. And suddenly, after his last attempt to escape, the police are informed of his existence. The hunt will start, at first slackly, and reach its climax when the Lieutenant of Police is vested with full power to carry it out. Hitherto we have known the priest only from the outside; now we begin to see things from his 'point of view'. Step by step he is reduced to utter abandonment; all doors are closed to him, as he is hunted down by the Lieutenant and the half-caste traitor who tries to get the price for his head. Twice, however, he escapes from the hands of the Lieutenant of Police, who does not know him, first in the village where his daughter lives, then in the prison of the Capital, when charged with the unlawful carrying of alcohol. It is an irony of fate that he should be allowed to attempt a third escape, which might have been successful, by entering a neighbouring state after a long walk across the mountains. But the enemy is close at his heels and still finds a way to stretch a hand across the border, to call him back to death. Enchained by his priesthood, printed upon him like a birth-mark, the whisky-priest is led to martyrdom.

A squat, grey-haired man walks up the street in front of the hotel, but Wilson cannot tell that this is one of those occasions one never forgets. Scobie the Just, the Deputy Commissioner of Police, the only officer trusted by his chief for special missions, admired by his pastor, Father Rank, is one of the few who have resisted the effects of the awful climate. He is even a good loser. Yet he is not liked at the Secretariat, because these very qualities seem to his colleagues to be a continuous personal reproach. We learn at the opening of his story that he will be passed over for promotion to the commissionership. His wife cannot get over this last disappointment and Scobie will be driven to borrow from Yusef, the Syrian, to send her for her health to South Africa. Fate

39

has struck. Within a few months, Scobie will be carried down the slippery slope that ends in suicide. Wilson, a special agent sent from London to investigate a case of diamond smuggling, falls in love with Louise. Jealous of Scobie, his wits sharpened by hatred, he scents something wrong in the relationship of Scobie and Yusef, and spies on Scobie, who while Louise is away in South Africa falls in love unawares with Helen Rolt. Scobie, watched by Wilson, blackmailed by Yusef, agrees to pass contraband diamonds. When Louise comes back, he cannot choose between the two women; he has to lie and commit sacrilegious communions to keep the truth from his wife and is pushed by Yusef to share responsibility for the murder of his boy, Ali. Hunted by Wilson and sick of giving pain, he sees no other issue than suicide. When in the end he is finally chosen for the commissionership, Scobie thinks bitterly: "All this need not have happened. If Louise had stayed I should never have loved Helen: I would never have been blackmailed by Yusef, never have committed that act of despair."

The web of destiny is woven around these men; subdued to its purpose, other characters are organized about them according to a definite pattern. A triangular relationship can be made out in all three novels and it becomes progressively more complex and skilful. In *Brighton Rock*, Pinkie is tied to two women, Ida and Rose, the good and the bad angel, both of them continuously opposed either directly or by contrast. In *The Power and the Glory*, the relationship is less clear, a more mysterious significance being conveyed in the opposition between Coral, the daughter according to the spirit, and

Brigitta, the daughter according to the flesh, and also the Lieutenant of Police, the whisky-priest's enemy. In *The Heart of the Matter*, a double triangle appears around Scobie, with Louise and Helen, Wilson and Yusef. Their opposition is introduced even into the construction of the novel. The First Book is devoted to Scobie and Louise; the Second to Scobie and Helen, while Wilson accounts entirely for the second part of both, and Yusef for at least one important scene in the first and third parts. The Third Book ties up the plot with the final intolerable situation.

Having demonstrated the main external factors in the destiny of these men and women, and analysed the structure of their environment and the chain of events leading them to their doom, we are now in a position to penetrate to the core of the drama. To do so we must try to enter into their minds, and, in the deep forest of their hearts, to snare the dangerous snake.

PART TWO

THE DRAMA OF FREEDOM

★

"The good that I would I do not: but the evil which I would not, that I do ... For I delight in the law of God after the inward man: but I see another law in my members, warring against the law of my mind, and bringing me into captivity to the law of sin which is in my members."

St Paul—EPISTLE TO THE ROMANS

"Parce que notre liberté est nous-mêmes, elle peut nous paraître à certaines heures inaccessible. Oui, tout se passe alors comme si un abîme étroit mais infranchissable nous séparait d'elle, comme si nous ne pouvions la joindre."

Gabriel Marcel—DU REFUS À L'INVOCATION

"There's another man within me that's angry with me."
Sir Thomas Browne (Epigraph to THE MAN WITHIN)

LOST IN A STRANGE world, unhappy, suffering from his plight, man questions his destiny, and in doing so becomes conscious of an interior division. He is existence and essence, a thinking and an empiric self. The working of his consciousness is felt as a dissociation of his being. This is the main theme of *The Man Within*. In this, his first novel, Greene deals openly with the mystery of man's personality and it is illuminating because it supplies us with a basis for the study of all his later characters, who no longer speculate on their nature but live according to it. Thought underlies action while it unfolds, but as an integral part of character, not as the object of contemplation.

Andrews "was, he knew, embarrassingly made up of two persons, the sentimental, bullying child and another more stern critic. If someone believed in me—but he did not believe in himself." Andrews is conscious of his failure to "exist", of his lack of personality: "Always while one part of him spoke, another part stood on one side and wondered 'Is this I who am speaking? Can I really exist like this?' . . . There was nothing in him but sentimentality and fear and cowardice, nothing in him but negatives. How could anyone believe in him if he did not even exist?" He cannot get below the surface of himself; his sincerity goes no further than a simple awareness of all

45

the tendencies warring in his mind, his secret impulses, the best and the worst. Greene's vision of man is close to that expressed by Louis Lavelle or Gabriel Marcel. Our self is given us only in the form of potentialities; these are revealed in our dreams, which we alone can know. Others judge us by what they see: "How could one judge a man, when all was said, but by his body and his private acts, not by dreams he followed in the world's eye?" All these elements which we perceive in ourselves are not the real person. True sincerity is a dynamic factor which enables us to discover in our "flickering personalities" an inner active self. And, in this process of discovering what we are, we at the same time create ourselves; choosing to be what we really are, beyond the passing impulse of the moment, we realize our potentialities, which until then have no positive value. Thus, by constant attention to the inner call and with the courage to answer it, even the coward may be turned into a hero, as Andrews suddenly perceived.

While we are limited and individualized by our destiny, we can and must accept it and, by so doing, become a person. This is where our freedom lies, in the power to respond to the situation we have been placed in. We are conditioned by our environment, our past, our nature too, but we can assume them, being simultaneously immanent and transcendent to history. Our attitude must be one of commitment, by which we accept to face our present, while assuming our past and preparing our future. Using our will, we choose and so orient our lives in the line of our destiny. Our situation is only the concrete material given us as a test; whether we reject it or identify ourselves with it, thereby surrendering to our determinism, we fail to use our freedom or debase it, and this is sin. Satan invades us, and our personality undergoes a process of complete disintegration, for the effect of sin is yet greater sin. We are the victims of its fatal rule.

Until we are truly attentive to the inner critic (and this calls for courage), we do not really exist. Andrews was able to catch a glimpse in Elizabeth of "the promise of his two selves at one, the peace which he had discovered sometimes in music". Later Bendrix, in *The End of the Affair*, is made aware of the same truth by Sarah, who comes closer to sanctity, for: "The saints, one would suppose, in a sense create themselves. They come alive. They are capable of the surprising act or word. They stand outside the plot, unconditioned by it. But we have to be pushed around. We have the obstinacy of non-existence."

Greene reveals with compassion the world of those who seem unable to stand outside the plot. His sympathy goes out to the most miserable of men, so weak that they cannot apply their will to free the "inward man" in them, those who are caught in the mud. To what degree, we wonder, can man's psychical constitution interfere with man's penetration by the grace of God? How far can such terms as free will and mortal sin be applied to those who drift like victims of an enormous wreck? The case of Pinkie, the whisky-priest and Scobie is much worse than that of Anthony Farrant, Raven and Arthur Rowe because "they know". They go consciously to their destruction and are brought "into captivity to the law of sin", beyond any apparent possibility of help. We come

47

to the heart of the great tragedy of freedom in which we
are all concerned.

II   PINKIE'S "LOST CHILDHOOD"

> *"In ancient shadows and twilights*
> *Where childhood had strayed,*
> *The world's great sorrows were born*
> *And its heroes were made.*
> *In the lost boyhood of Judas*
> *Christ was betrayed."*
>
> A.E. *'Germinal'* (Quoted in THE LOST CHILDHOOD)

THE THEME OF lost innocence, of the influence of our
early impressions upon our later behaviour, of children
doomed to an early knowledge of corruption and evil, is
recurrent in Greene's work. Pinkie, however, seems to
be the strongest actualization of this obsession which in
Brighton Rock becomes for the first time the principal
theme of a whole novel. He belongs to the host of juvenile
delinquents who bear witness to the shortcomings of our
social order. Andrews, already, had suffered from the
strain of a childhood spent between a ruthless father and
too good a mother. Anthony Farrant in *England Made
Me* never outgrew the dreams and the need for protection
of his boyhood. Philip, in *The Basement Room*, was
frightened when life fell on him with savagery and he
extricated himself "from life, from love, from Baines,
with a merciless egotism". Raven in *A Gun for Sale*
exclaims: "This isn't a world I'd bring children into . . .
three minutes in bed or against a wall, and then a lifetime
for the one that's born. . . . It was like you carry a load

48

around you; you are born with some of it because of what your father and mother were and their fathers. . . . Then when you are a kid the load gets bigger, all the things you need to do and can't; and then all the things you do." Children are too sensitive and vulnerable; they are not strong enough to carry the load placed upon their narrow shoulders; they betray the truth perceived, harden into indifference or irresponsibility or hate, or die in their knowledge, like Else and Coral, like the pale child and Scobie's daughter. Closer to Pinkie are the Lieutenant of Police in *The Power and the Glory* and Raven in *A Gun for Sale*, with their hatred of religion and avoidance of sex. Pinkie, an incarnation of nearly "perfect evil walking the world", is also close to Hall in *England Made Me*, Willie Hilfe in *The Ministry of Fear*, Fred in 'A Drive in the Country', Blacker in 'A Hint of an Explanation', and Harry Lime in *The Third Man*, whose reckless enterprises are sustained by the supernatural power of the Devil.

Pinkie is hardly more than a child, saddled prematurely with adult responsibilities. Under his apparently invincible strength, an immense weakness lies, a fundamental fear that compels him to refrain from getting entangled with the reality of life and suffering. His asceticism—no drink, no cigarettes, no women—is only one way of escaping the horror which had been the fundamental experience of the young child: a knowledge of poverty, hate, and the "Saturday night movements"— the "game"—lowering man to the level of an animal. The image constantly recurs like an obsession in his dreams and thoughts, and takes on a particular significance when he reaches puberty and begins to feel the prick of desire.

This early awareness of misery has given birth to a repugnance to and fear of life, to a desire for vacancy, a monstrous solitude, and egotism. We hear Pinkie make this strange confession to Dallow who does not understand: " 'When I was a kid, I swore I'd be a priest. . . . They know what's what. They keep away'—his whole mouth and jaw loosened: he might have been going to weep: he beat out wildly with his hands towards the window—Woman Found Drowned, Two-Valve, *Married Passion*, the horror—'from this'." Such was the "good temptation" felt by the choir-boy whose memory later on would still be filled with sacred music. . . . But the child has grown up and the load of misery has grown too; the call to priesthood was never answered, and Pinkie developed a terrible hatred of the world and of his fellow men, as a refuge against the cracked bell ringing, the cement playground, the cruelty of other children. He gives way to sadistic instincts. Here again Greene's own experience can be adduced to explain the fiction. The horrifying cruelty he ascribes to Pinkie seems related to the confession made in *Journey Without Maps*: "Like a revelation, when I was fourteen, I realized the pleasure of cruelty; I wasn't interested any longer in walks on commons, in playing cricket on the beach. There was a girl lodging close by I wanted to do things to. . . . I could think about pain as something desirable and not as something dreaded. It was as if I had discovered the way to enjoy life was to appreciate pain." Pinkie had made the same discovery; his repressed sexuality is perverted

50

into a sad but cruel joy at the infliction of pain—first with a pair of dividers, later in more dangerous ways.

Then Kite appears; his role seems to be important in the Boy's destiny. The man who picks him up alone on the pier, and brings him back to Frank's, will be for the boy a father. But what a world it is into which he brings him! Pinkie's dreams will again yield the deep meaning of his hero-worship for Kite. He is, as it were, a new boy and sick with fear of the other children coming "towards him with a purpose". He needed Kite. " 'Such tits', Kite said, and put a razor in his hand. He knew then what to do: they only needed to be taught once that he would stop at nothing, that there were no rules." Kite had freed him from his world of fear, religious law compelling him to be good; he had been given a tool to escape from the misery, "worth murdering a world". Thus were born the reckless revolt, the worldly ambition to outpace his rival, Colleoni, and the infernal pride for his successful enterprises.

This is about as far as we can go in reconstructing Pinkie's past, from his own thoughts and dreams. Kite is no longer there to protect him and tell him what to do; but Pinkie is going to take up his inheritance, and first avenge Kite's death in the St Pancras waiting-room by the murder of Hale. Hell lies about him in his "infancy", driving him on to his end within a few weeks. The devils inhabit his soul; following his evil tendencies—the only habits he has ever developed—and having discarded all the rules, he is now enslaved to the law of sin and on the slippery slope to complete self-destruction and hell. He is gradually hunted to his last refuge by fear and the terrible

compelling need for personal safety: the fear of thinking
that he may be done for, which he confesses to Dallow,
whose dumb physical strength he needs in order to con-
firm his faith in his own powers and cunning; the fear
of seeing "an end to the great future", when the Inspec-
tor takes him to the charge-room, simply to advise him
to clear out of Brighton; the fear of losing his grip, of
Ida pursuing him, robbing him of safety; the fear of pain
and death when Colleoni's men attack him; the fear
seizing him when Spicer, whom he had supposed dead, is
heard on the floor above, which leads him to murder him
a second time. After the wedding-night, and the victory
over the sexual impotence he had experienced with
Sylvie, his pride utters a cry of triumph: he has gradu-
ated in the last human shame. "He had a sense that he
would never be scared again: running down from the
track he had been afraid, afraid of pain and more afraid
of damnation—of the sudden and unshriven death. Now
it was as if he was damned already and there was nothing
more to fear ever again." So he thinks, but there is to be
no peace for him; the fear of drowning overwhelms him
in a nightmare the same night and he wakes to realize
with horror that there is no end to what they have just
done. Our last sight of him is that of a "schoolboy flying
in panic and pain, scrambling over a fence, running on
. . . whipped away into zero—nothing".

The habit of hatred and pride prevents him from
answering the faint inner voice which tells him of his
weakness and tries to call him back to another way of life.
Each time he refuses the warning and gives way to
cruelty, miserable in the knowledge of being driven by an

52

interior necessity much further than he had ever con-
templated, until he even regrets for a while Hale's
murder: "He deserved what he got, but if I'd known how
it would go maybe I'd have let him live." The child's pair
of dividers have been discarded for the razor, but greater
evil is to come. He feels a terrible joy at the pain inflicted
on Spicer. His sadistic cruelty will plan the darkest act of
all; his complete escape from responsibility, from the
"infringement of other people's lives" had been his
strength, but life has bound him by Rose's love and
obliged him to take a responsibility which, in his selfishness, he refuses to assume. To his rising pity and tenderness, another word answers: "Myself". If Rose were dead,
"no more human contacts, other people's emotion washing at the brain—he would be free again: nothing to think
about but himself". Each surrender corresponds to one
more step down: "the empty tenement and then the
seven devils worse than the first", until his mind staggers.
The suicide pact, devised to make Rose kill herself two
days after their marriage, is the worst and last horror
bred by the mad brain of the lost child. "You're crazy",
Dallow says.

When Pinkie hates Rose and inflicts pain, he is in fact
hating and hurting himself, because she represents his lost
goodness, his true self. He revenges himself on her for his
own failure. His evil calls for her goodness. The power
that compels him to accept the eternal damnation of both
of them as the price of his temporal safety is satanic. As
Bendrix perceived in *The End of the Affair*: "If there is a
God who uses us and makes his saints out of such
material as we are, the devil too may have his ambitions;

he may dream of training even such a person as myself into being his saint, ready with borrowed fanaticism to destroy love wherever we find it." It is Pinkie who is driven in the end to suicide—the desperate issue to which his friend Annie Collins had surrendered on the railway line. His death will be by drowning, as he had foreseen in his dream. He returns to the "annihilating eternity", the vacancy from which he had come and which he desired, flying from time with all the clocks striking in his hell with terrifying precision to hasten him to his end. For Andrews also in *The Man Within* "time was here in the cottage. Clocks ticked and hands went round as everywhere else in the world. He had a sense of time rushing past him, rushing like a Gadarene swine to destruction." This sense of time rushing past is particularly strong in *Brighton Rock*, the experiences like love, beauty, peace, which give a gleam of eternity to the passing moment, being reduced almost to nothing here, at least from Pinkie's point of view; only in the end, in the presence of death, time stretches, and the clocks of Brighton stop in the dark, in the huge disaster.

Pinkie's story fills us with horror; to reach such depths of sin and crime shocks the imagination. If anyone is damned, it is Pinkie. And then we are overcome, as Greene himself is, by pity for this criminal who is only a child, the victim of his environment, of fate, of his hatred and pride, whose misery is immense. Greene stresses all the factors pressing upon him. He is bound by his experience, which has made him unfit to conceive anything but hell: "Credo in unum Satanum." He feels, in a moment of awareness, that he has not had his

54

chance and "seen his glimpse of heaven if it was only a crack between the Brighton walls . . . Rose might be it—but the brain could not conceive." Pinkie explains to Rose: "It's in the blood. Perhaps when they christened me, the holy water didn't take. I never howled the devil out."

III   THE CORRUPT PRIEST

> "*Every priest was hunted down or shot, except one who existed for ten years in the forests and the swamps, venturing out only at night; his few letters, I was told, recorded an awful sense of impotence—to live in constant danger and yet be able to do so little; it hardly seemed worth the horror.*"

> "*I asked about the priest in Chiapas who had fled. 'Oh,' he said, 'he was just what we call a whisky-priest.' He had taken one of his sons to be baptized, but the priest was drunk and would insist on naming him Brigitta. He was little loss, poor man.*"
>
> THE LAWLESS ROADS

THE CATHOLIC PRIEST, as spokesman of the Church's teachings, plays an important part in Greene's work. He appears as the anonymous priest trying to bring comfort to Rose in *Brighton Rock*; as the pious narrow-minded Father Clay of Bemba; as Father Rank nearly breaking down in front of Scobie, admitting his failure to help, ministering to his widow after his suicide; and again as Father Crompton in *The End of the Affair*. He turns up especially in the presence of death as an earnest of God's mercy and of the life to come, and to administer the

Sacraments. But his dignity as priest is not necessarily linked with personal holiness. When we are permitted to penetrate into his private life and to see him as he is, he generally turns out to be little better than any other man.

The Power and the Glory is a striking illustration of how a priest can be subjected to temptation and still retain his sacred dignity unimpaired, whatever degree of corruption he may have reached. Here a priest has the leading role. For all that, he is another human failure and a greater sinner, on account of his vows, than ordinary men; but he dies for his faith like Father Pro who was shot in Mexico in 1927. We can reconstruct his past, like Pinkie's, from his dreams and memories. Strangely similar attitudes of mind are revealed by this method. First as concerns his vocation. His childhood, unlike Pinkie's, had been happy in Carmen, where his father was a store-keeper, but already the misery of the peons had struck him and had bred fear in his heart. Life had caught him, weak and unable to carry its load; and he had looked for some easier way to security than the calculations and risks of a business career. To the child there seemed no easier way than the priesthood. "It had been a happy childhood, except that he had been afraid of too many things, and had hated poverty like a crime: he had believed that when he was a priest he would be rich and proud—that was called having a vocation." And he had become the complacent, successful priest, respected by his parishioners in Conception, comparatively innocent, not used to liquor, a fat youngish man enjoying the sound of his own voice, trying out vulgar jokes, moved by ambition, not humble like Padre José,

56

a peon by birth, whose hands shook at the Elevation of the Host. "He was not content to remain all his life the priest of a not very large parish", but knew how to manage his business successfully. He was one of those who motivated the hatred of the Lieutenant of Police and the revolt of the poor.

And then came the evil days, the long ten years' ordeal. The desire to postpone action dominated the fear, until he realized that he was the only priest left in the State. He felt suddenly glad to be freed from the last man who could disapprove of him, from any rules but his own. Ironically, he found himself taking the easy way, as he had in his choice of vocation. "I didn't have to think about anybody's opinion any more. The people— they didn't worry me. They liked me." His ambition becomes a devilish pride. When Kite went away, Pinkie was left alone with his seventeen years' experience of Brighton slum life, with no rules, and with the urge to commit ever darker crimes; the priest, alone too in the Godless State, with no one to ask advice from, is gradually led, surrender by surrender, to mortal sin and to the complete disintegration of his being. He had not taken into account his fundamental weakness and fear of pain. After ten years of this kind of life, when the final hunt begins to close all the ways of escape against him, he considers the immeasurable distance a man travels; nobody but himself would recognize as the same man the face in the photograph posted in the Police charge-room. "The years behind him were littered with surrenders— feast days and fast days and days of abstinence had been the first to go: then he had ceased to trouble more than occasionally about his breviary—and finally he had left it behind altogether at the port in one of his periodic attempts at escape. Then the altar stone went—too dangerous to carry with him. He had no business to say Mass without it: he was probably liable to suspension, but penalties of the ecclesiastical kind began to seem unreal in a state where the only penalty was the civil one of death. The routine of his life, like a dam, was cracked and forgetfulness came dribbling in, wiping out this and that. Five years ago he had given way to despair—the unforgivable sin—and he was going back now to the scene of his despair with a curious lightening of the heart. For he had got over despair too. He was a bad priest, he knew it: they had a word for his kind—a whisky-priest, but every failure dropped out of sight and mind: somewhere they accumulated in secret—the rubble of his failures. One day they would choke up, he supposed, altogether the source of grace. Until then he carried on, with spells of fear, weariness, with a shamefaced lightness of heart."

Weariness and fear render him powerless in the face of the events shaping his destiny; he lets himself go to pieces in a thoroughly unheroic fashion. Pain and suffering are forced on him, not voluntarily accepted. Compelled by his duty as a priest, he follows the child into the dark interior to succour the dying woman, "as though unwillingly he had been summoned to an occasion he couldn't pass by". Shaken by a "tiny rage", he drinks some brandy to get a little courage. He weeps from sheer exhaustion when the man in the hut asks him to hear the people of the community in confession. "Oh, let them

58

come. Let them come", he cries angrily. "I am your servant." An immense weariness invades him every time he
thinks that death is at hand and he must still go on living.
"God had decided. He had to go on with life, go on making decisions, acting on his own advice, making plans."
When he escapes at last across the border, he finds himself being drawn back to his old life, as if his experience
of hardship had taught him nothing. Once again he is
bargaining in his patronizing voice about the price of
baptism, once again he is respected and successful, as in
the old days, and conscious of the returning habit of
piety, but apparently unable to control himself, unable
even to throw off the habit of drink. "He told himself—in
time it will be all right, I shall pull up, I only ordered
three bottles this time. They will be the last I'll ever
drink, I won't need drink there—he knew he lied." He
has to be forced to go back to the dying man to whom he
cannot refuse confession.

He is constantly aware of the extent of his degradation,
of being in a state of mortal sin, of carrying hell about
with him, of evil running "like malaria" in his veins and
filling his dreams with satanic images. "He remembered
a dream he had had of a big grassy arena lined with the
statues of the saints—but the saints were alive, they
turned their eyes this way and that, waiting for something. He waited, too, with an awful expectancy: bearded
Peters and Pauls, with Bibles pressed to their breasts,
watched some entrance behind his back he couldn't see—
it had the menace of a beast. Then a marimba began to
play, tinkly and repetitive, a firework exploded, and
Christ danced into the arena—danced and postured with

59

a bleeding painted face, up and down, up and down, grimacing like a prostitute, smiling and suggestive." But the whisky-priest seems unable to repent because he has got beyond despair. "The mystery became too great, a damned man putting God into the mouths of men: an odd sort of servant that, for the devil." Whenever he feels death approaching he attempts an act of contrition, but that "was the fallacy of the death-bed repentance—penitence was the fruit of long training and discipline". He is left with only an imperfect contrition and his fear, temporarily overcome by brandy, but shaking him at the moment of danger and always overwhelming him in the end. Even his death looks like one more failure. "He was held up by two policemen, but you could tell that he was doing his best—it was only that his legs were not fully under his control." It was thus that he had appeared to the dentist at their first meeting, with the "dwarfed dignity of people afraid of a little pain and yet sitting down with some firmness in his chair".

Chained to priesthood which he had originally chosen as a way of escape, placed in a situation it would have needed a saint to accept and cope with, this poor, corrupt man, who is little better than a thief, finds his vocation at the eleventh hour and with the help of brandy. In the end he is allowed to realize "that it would have been quite easy to have been a saint. It would have needed a little self-restraint and a little courage"—and this had not been granted him. For want of courage and self-discipline, he had failed throughout his life to keep the secret appointment made for him.

60

IV   SCOBIE'S "TERRIBLE IMPOTENT FEELING OF RESPONSIBILITY AND PITY"

"What an absurd thing it was to expect happiness in a world so full of misery."

THE HEART OF THE MATTER

"He wanted to warn them—don't pity me. Pity is cruel. Pity destroys. Love isn't safe when pity's prowling round."

THE MINISTRY OF FEAR

GREENE SHOWS EVEN profounder psychological insight in the character of Scobie, the most complex of his heroes. The whisky-priest was the product of abnormal and violent circumstances. Pinkie was a lost child inhabited by seven devils. Scobie is the relatively common type of the unsatisfied, middle-aged man of good will but weak character, unable to face his responsibilities. He also poses for a Catholic the problem of suicide much more directly than it was by Pinkie.

Greene would appear to have been haunted by Scobie for a long while. In *It's a Battlefield* we find the first clear hint of what will later be Scobie's problem. A Police Commissioner, appointed to London after long service in the East, suffers from spells of disgust at the uselessness of his work for a social order in which he does not believe. Prompted by an obscure pity and compassion to help its victims, he is periodically tempted to give way to his death-wish as a means of escape from his profound dissatisfaction and from his fear of retirement. But these feelings do not dominate his mind as they ultimately dominate Scobie's in the tropical climate of the Coast; he never actually yields to his impulses and is always

61

brought back from his dark thoughts by a sense of duty and by the satisfaction of performing the job for which he is paid. But the Police Commissioner is a bachelor with no experience of the disenchantment of a married couple, pretending to love each other when in fact only pity remains. The association of love with pity is often found in Greene's work: in *It's a Battlefield* in Conrad Drover's love for Milly and his desire to spare her anything he could; in Mr Lever of 'A Chance for Mr Lever' who "continued to write the only kind of lies he'd ever told Emily, the lies which comforted"; in the Fellows of *The Power and the Glory*; in D. of *The Confidential Agent* who cannot make out whether his feeling for Rose Cullen is pity or love; in Rollo in *The Third Man* who is touched by Anna's face—a face "for wear".

Even more important for the light it throws on the genesis of Scobie is *The Ministry of Fear*. Arthur Rowe, the mercy-killer, gives way to the "horrible and horrifying emotion of pity". His precarious calm is broken by the feeling that people suffer, and in a moment of acute feeling of this kind he poisons his wife (whom he loves) in order to avoid the pain of seeing her suffering. By the same process Greene used for Pinkie and the whisky-priest, we are allowed to trace the origin of this attitude to the acute and sickly sensitivity of a child who could not bear to see a rat in pain. Pushed by remorse, Rowe even gets to the point when he thinks of himself as another rat to be killed; and then he gets involved with Anna Hilfe, though their happiness will always be blurred by the fear of their mutual secret being found out.

We know nothing of Scobie's childhood, except that

62

"at a preparatory school he had been given a prize—a copy of *Allan Quatermain*—for keeping a diary throughout one summer holiday". We know from Greene's confession in 'The Lost Childhood' what dreams of a journey to Africa can be roused in the mind of a child by this book. It is probably meant to account for Scobie's attraction to the Coast and to symbolize his own voyage through dark, desolate territories, to despair and death. From Arthur Rowe's story it is easy to reconstruct the experiences which probably formed the attitudes of his mature years. Two important facts about Scobie's past are, however, supplied. His destiny was conditioned for ever by the awful vow made during the marriage ceremony at Ealing, when he had "sworn that he would at least always see to it that [Louise] was happy". But who can guarantee love for ever? There lies the intrinsic risk of marriage which Scobie took when he became a Catholic to marry his wife; he had committed himself to a choice determining his future. Fourteen years later, little was left of his original love but the element of pity in it and the sense of responsibility, which increased as he drifted further away from Louise. The feelings change but the vows remain. The second important event which clearly influenced Scobie's attitude deeply was his only daughter's death in childhood. He had been spared seeing her die and had been left with a strong sense of guilt because he had not taken his share of the load his child and his wife had borne. This is evidently intended by the author to increase Scobie's pity for Louise, and this brings us to his central problem.

Scobie's unusually acute sensitivity to the huge misery

of the world is combined with a sense of responsibility towards it and an immense longing for peace. He is good, unable to inflict pain even when necessary, or to witness it. He is one of those who are "trapped and betrayed" by their virtues until they are hunted into an impasse, for "courage smashes a cathedral, endurance lets a city starve, pity kills". Although Scobie means to give them happiness, he only succeeds in betraying his wife, his mistress and his God. Life always reproduces the same pattern; in Scobie's case it is woven around his own constant response to it, which is his sense of pity. This is the key to Scobie's personality. Greene gives us in Scobie's story one of the most intuitive and understanding analyses of this ambiguous emotion.

Can pity really be called a virtue or must it be considered as "the worst passion of all"? Or is it perhaps only a distortion or rather a simplification of the passion of love? Pity is one of the harmonics of love in the presence of suffering, but not love itself. This difference is illustrated by the attitude of Buddhists who know only compassion but not love. This sublime tenderness is not to be applied to man himself but to his misery; it is concerned with misery in general rather than with the individual miserable human being, and is to be considered not as an end, but as a way or a method to reach detachment. Pity is not a substitute for love; when separated from it, it is ultimately destructive, a negative sharing of a failure, whereas love is creative. Love, in Berdyaev's words, is "an eternal affirmation" of human personality. Love is fire and must often hurt in order to achieve its ends. Pity is the easy way, an escape for the weak, who cannot face truth directly or tolerate any impediment to their self-centred peace. It is the flaw in Scobie's strength; sentimental pity will drive him to his own destruction, first to professional delinquency, then to adultery, murder (of Ali) and sacrilegious communions, and finally to suicide.

One of the forms which Scobie's pity takes is the comforting lie, which postpones unhappiness by pretending to ignore the truth. He lies to himself by destroying any reminder of worry or pain, even the picture of his own dead child. "He had cut down his own needs to a minimum, photographs were put away in drawers, the dead were put out of mind: a razor-strop, a pair of rusty handcuffs for decoration: but one still has one's eyes, he thought, one's ears." His presence at the death of the child in Pende is an atonement for his absence from his daughter's death-bed. "It seemed after all that one never really missed a thing. To be a human being one had to drink the cup." There is no escaping the misery. Scobie also lies to his wife in order to put off their mutual misery, and to protect her, although he knows that no one can arrange another's happiness. He dismisses the possibility of improving her or of bringing out her good qualities; instead he pretends that he still loves her as much as ever and makes a show of satisfying all her immediate demands. She suffers from his pity; she would have needed strength and real love to develop her true self. As it is, she is aware of the lies and is not even glad at having her passage to South Africa arranged, for in her heart she knows that it is not the best solution of their problem. For a while they speak the truth to each other. "That's your conscience," she said sadly, "your

65

sense of duty. You've never loved anyone since Catherine died." In himself too he is aware of his responsibility in having made her what she is. He discovers that she loves him, that she is "someone of human stature with her own sense of responsibility, not simply the object of his care and kindness". This failure leads to a separation resembling a divorce, which leaves a place vacant for someone else to fill.

The whole process of dangerous pity, concealing the approach of desire but outlasting it, is reproduced, albeit in different terms, with Helen. Like Louise, she rebukes Scobie for his pity and comforting lies. "Pity smouldered like decay at his heart. . . . He knew from experience how passion died away, and how love went but pity always stayed." He is bound by "the command to stay, to love, to accept responsibility, to lie". More lies become necessary when Louise returns, along with repeated sacrilegious communions, until he feels "his whole personality crumble with the slow disintegration of lies".

Marcel Moré in his essay, 'Les deux Holocaustes de Scobie', stresses the neurotic aspect of Scobie's character, as revealed in his sense of guilt, his obsession with lies and the signs of suicidal mania in his careful early preparation for the actual suicide. This is particularly apparent in the episode of Pemberton's suicide in Bemba; the event seems to bring out an unconscious but existing tendency in Scobie, and the idea of suicide haunts his dreams repeatedly as a possible escape from his problems. The letter signed 'Dicky', left by Pemberton for his father, becomes associated in Scobie's fevered brain with his own nickname, Ticki. The subject is reverted to from

66

time to time and particularly in the scene at the Fellows's when discussion turns on this tragic issue with an intolerable levity. Scobie, who is vitally concerned in it, is touched to the depths of his being and it is then that he unconsciously chooses the mode of his own suicide. He is ready for the unforgivable sin. Every wound festers in the humid atmosphere and the slow corruption deprives him of any way out of despair. He has entered a territory from which there is no return: "It seemed to him that he had rotted so far that it was useless to make any effort. God was lodged in his body and his body was corrupting outwards from that seed." Others suffer or die just because he exists; and his suicide—his last lie—so cunningly concealed from Louise and Helen, is also his last act of pity for those he loves—Louise and Helen and God too—and to whom he can only bring pain. His final decision is made in the belief that the only way to spare God from further pain is to destroy himself altogether. Scobie has lost the sense of trust. One may question whether he ever had it: his extraordinary sense of responsibility seems to exclude the possibility that others can have one too. This is what Louise and Helen felt. His act of despair is an act of spiritual pride, for which all the occasions when he trusted no one but himself were a preparation. When he opened the letter of the Portuguese captain against the strictest orders, Scobie had already exercised his own imperfect judgment. Later he will not trust God to take care of those whom he loves.

Scobie's obsessions, his failure to take the decision which one side of him always knew was the right one—to hand over the letter to the censors, to abandon his attempts to send Louise away, and later to clean up, abandon Helen and confess—his propensity for self-deception, all point to a fundamental weakness, if not a mental disease which, in conjunction with the corrupting atmosphere around him, are, as it were, symptoms of the sickness that destroyeth in the noon-day.

V   THE "TERROR OF LIFE"

> *"Now I have sunk so deep that surely I've reached the bottom. I could kill myself . . . He felt no fear of death, but a terror of life, of going on soiling himself and repenting and soiling himself again. There was, he felt, no escape. He had no will left."*
>
> THE MAN WITHIN

> *"It is impossible to go through life without trust; that is to be imprisoned in the worst cell of all, oneself."*
>
> THE MINISTRY OF FEAR

ANDREWS, THE FIRST-BORN of Greene's characters, was also the first of them to experience the "terror of life". Kenneth Allott and Miriam Farris, in *The Art of Graham Greene*, consider it to be the motive force of Greene's work. We have seen how this emotion, linked with a longing for peace, was responsible, in others besides Andrews, for a recurrent desire to escape. We have detected in Pinkie's and the whisky-priest's childhood and in Scobie's life the fundamental experience which accounts for this attitude, developed from a basic awareness of the huge misery of the world, the terrible plight of man, and "the innumerable necessary evils of which

68

life [is] made up". Hell is about us, pain is everywhere, even the innocent share in the common lot. Pinkie, the whisky-priest and Scobie touch us because of their awareness of evil and because of their own suffering. But whereas a child recognizes evil but does not know how to react to it, an adult adopts an attitude, which he will continue to hold even when the original vision has become dim. Pinkie, just out of childhood, is led to revolt and to indulge in sensual cruelty and merciless hate (according to the way of the world about him), but he cannot avoid the fear of his own rejected past assailing him. Scobie differs from him in that his sense of suffering does not bring him peace; his response to experience—an overwhelming pity extended to all the miseries of the world—seems the opposite of Pinkie's hate; but we learn that even compassion can turn into a source of corruption. The whisky-priest, having elected for a safe way of escape, is later by this very choice brought to an understanding of the redeeming virtues of suffering and so to true love. Yet the fundamental fear remains, the physical wincing under pain, the psychological reluctance to act and take responsibility, the metaphysical awe of God and of the risk of damnation.

We shall come back to this problem of evil and suffering, a problem which our intelligence cannot grasp. It is one of the profound mysteries with which we are faced in our daily life. The possibility of using suffering for a greater good does not stand to reason. There is, it would seem, a dark response to suffering, which can turn into a "dark and incalculable force" and lead to damnation; yet nobody can judge the man who is so exhausted by his

69

load that he refuses to carry it any longer, or who curses all pain. Nevertheless our attitude towards evil and towards the painful division wrought by sin in the world must not be one of mere resignation. As Berdyaev has said: "From the remotest times man has longed to be delivered from the intolerable burden of suffering and from servitude to evil. Man's greatest spiritual flights are associated with this longing."

This yearning for peace, however, can sometimes disguise the unheroic desire to avoid the effort required to create our true self: "The renouncement of the personality is one of the ways of seeking deliverance from suffering and evil . . . for personality implies pain, and its realization brings suffering. The labour of engendering the personality implies sacrifice, but not the renunciation of the personality." This is where so many people fail; they oppose an interior inertia to the only real demand made upon them, and by so doing betray themselves and undermine their very freedom. This appears to be the problem of Greene's characters. Their burden becomes so unbearable that they break down from sheer impotence. Instead of responding dynamically to life, they are afraid to commit themselves and, instead, accuse fate. They are lost in the end because they believe there is nothing they can do. Gabriel Marcel has analysed the attitude of 'unhope' of man tormented by deadly anxiety and worry for his 'belongings'. In such a case all initiative is paralysed, and we exist in a state of stagnation and corruption, involving ourselves in a process of self-destruction. In some of Greene's characters, this is accompanied by an element of masochism.

70

Pinkie is haunted by the idea that his past conditions him; but it is because he rejects it that it turns out to be ineluctable. Scobie, unable to face the consequences of the vows made years ago in the church at Ealing, finally betrays them. It is not enough to face the present by a choice; one has to assume the past and all the consequences of this choice; and Scobie knows this but fails in the task. Like Pinkie, he gives way to despair, the extreme failure, suicide. The future appears to them completed before it is even lived, because of their inability to oppose a dynamic courage to fate. "There's a proverb, you know, about the end is the beginning. When I was born I was sitting here with you drinking whisky, knowing . . ." The whisky-priest also lacks the courage necessary to do anything but let himself be led according to the occasion; he fails to prove equal to his priesthood and gives way to mortal sin, though he is miraculously saved from despair.

By this reluctance to act, the constant debate between man's two selves is perverted into a destructive self-consideration. Like Narcissus contemplating his own image, man finds himself shut into "the worst cell of all" —himself. Pinkie is so muddled that he is unable even to conceive good. Scobie mistakes the voice of the tempting devil for his duty and can no more draw a line between good and evil in his thoughts than he can in the police cases he has to deal with. Both lose all control of their destiny. The case of the whisky-priest is different because, however far he may stray, he still carries on and finally answers a mysterious call and is not found wanting. The only way out of the lowest circle of fate is to

71

forget our own problems; we find ourselves when we open our hearts to other destinies.

The opposition between a passive and (ultimately) self-centred attitude of 'constancy' towards men and an unselfish and 'creative fidelity' (in the sense in which Gabriel Marcel uses the term) is the clue to the failure and solitude of Greene's characters. We have seen how Pinkie, by his terror of getting involved, is denied the possibility of life and creation; he is doomed to complete destruction because he refuses to trust anybody but himself. The whisky-priest and Scobie both committed themselves to a choice determining their lives. Each had pledged himself to the future and one may well wonder to what extent it is possible to make such a pledge, in view of the possibility of changing circumstances and, accordingly, of changing feelings. To be truly and 'creatively' faithful, a man must not only keep his engagement but also take into account possible development in his life, to be at the same time steady of purpose and flexible, for fear of betrayal or of a formal and rigid 'constancy'. The choice is made once for all and must never be questioned again; a mode of life is developed and orientated accordingly in a given direction. "All other possibilities, barred or rejected, [are] thereby dismissed as temptation." The pledge must also be an act of trust in another person, who is not to be considered only as the object of one's commitment but as a partner in the act. The case of Scobie now becomes clearer. In him the ways of evil are more dangerous because less apparent, and there is a greater delusive cunning in the approach of his enemy. He is too weak to resist. His apparent fidelity to his wife was in fact already a betrayal; as we have said, constancy is not fidelity nor pity love. His life has not been deeply orientated by his pledge; in his own eyes the contradictory promise made later to Helen binds him as much. He is unfaithful also to another promise, this time made to God: never to give up hope, which is the extreme form of trust, and faith, which is the extreme form of fidelity. Pinkie and Scobie give way to despair, but the whisky-priest, as we shall see, is saved by his fidelity to the essential.

For it is ultimately to this failure of fidelity to God that all sins can be assigned. And Pinkie, the whisky-priest and Scobie are sinners. To them—even to Pinkie—the lamentation of St Paul can be applied: "The good that I would I do not; but the evil which I would not that I do." There is a kind of fatality in the law of sin, warring in man against the Love of God. To what extent can these men so weak even in their good will be considered as responsible sinners? Are they victims of an obsession or possessed of the devil? Greene does not say. In their immense desire for peace we recognize the weariness denounced by Bernanos, which we have all experienced: "The exhaustion, the dejection, the collection of disgust at the bottom of the soul, the impurity, the defilement. . . . Weariness without as within, the immersion of weariness, the sin, the stigma, the curse of weariness (the weariness, the agony, the sharing of the universal shame of a wasted world, of man's betrayal of the world), a kind of poisoning of one's being." We cannot suppose that any man is entirely denied some measure of freedom; it only seems inaccessible sometimes because freedom is of our

73

essence; and there lies the tragedy: "In as much as we are free we are liable to betray ourselves and to see our salvation in this betrayal; and this is what is really tragic in our situation." But there lies the hope too, for no one can imagine the "depth of the riches both of the wisdom and knowledge of God! How unsearchable are his judgments, and his ways past finding out!"

PART THREE

THE POWER AND THE GLORY

★

"It was for this world that Christ had died: the more evil you saw and heard about you, the greater glory lay around the death; it was too easy to die for what was good or beautiful . . . it needed a God to die for the half-hearted and the corrupt."

"That is why I tell you that heaven is here: this is a part of heaven just as pain is a part of pleasure."

THE POWER AND THE GLORY

I   GOD, THE MAIN ACTOR OF THE DRAMA

"Then came . . . a moment in time but not like a
moment of time,
A moment in time but time was made through that
moment: for without the meaning there is no time, and
that moment of time gave the meaning."

T. S. *Eliot*, THE ROCK

ABOVE THE WASTE LAND and the circles of hell where man
is imprisoned, above the evil world still ruled by the law
of sin, a presence hovers, unseen at first and felt only as
nostalgia or as a vacancy in the heart. It is a vacancy
which Greene's lawless heroes vainly try to fill. "In the
beginning God created the world" . . . "Waste and void.
Waste and void. And darkness was upon the face of the
deep." The spirit of God still moves upon the face of the
world, but few are they who watch for him to pass over.
And yet the only escape from the grip of the seven devils
and from the terror of life is in him. The world about us
is a fallen world and man, an impotent creature crushed
by forces too great for him to withstand, falls again and
again in spite of his good intentions. Time is the measure
of our painful progress through this waste land. And yet
time has been redeemed and the world is no longer at the
mercy of the fallen angel. Man is not only doomed to sin
but is also capable of salvation. At the intersection of the
world and what is not the world, at the centre of history,
the Cross on which God died stands for ever, relieving
creation of its burden, opposing grace to sin, defeating
the Prince of this World. But even while the issue is

77

secure and the victory established once for all, the struggle continues in time and through time.

Man is split between supernatural forces while the great conflict between God and Satan rages in the world and more deeply in his own heart. When all is said, God is the principal actor in Greene's tragedies, the 'third man' we unconsciously seek. Between the lines of his detective stories another story is being told, and told more and more openly in the trilogy with which we are here concerned. The description of the complete failure of man left to his own devices, of his miserable condition, of his evil works, is intended as a tribute to the power and the glory of the Living God. For "where sin abounded grace did much more abound". The greater the failure of man, the greater the mercy of God. Greene himself has said that his purpose, like François Mauriac's, in choosing the weakest, the most abandoned human beings as material for his creative imagination, was to throw a brighter light on God's infinite mercy and on his power to turn even evil—'etiam peccata'—into good. In this, he recalls the revelations of St Augustine and of the mystics, who, like Juliana of Norwich, comfort themselves with the knowledge that "Sin is behovely, but all shall be well, and all shall be well, and all manner of thing shall be well"; that evil is the way of the world but love the way of God, "which love was never slacked nor ever shall be".

The God of Greene's later novels is not an abstract entity, a philosophical concept corresponding to a notion grasped only by our intelligence. He essentially *is* or *exists* as a living person. He is the God of the Bible,

78

making himself known to his people and speaking to
them through his servants; a jealous God teaching them
to obey his commandments and chastising them for their
backslidings. He is the God who works through history
and expects an answer to his promises and to his ordin-
ances. And he is also the God of the mystics, revealed
directly to the heart of man in an intimate relation as
between one person and another. In him a new meaning
is given to everything: natural signs are inverted so that
what was negative can be made positive. Human failures
as well as human potentialities are turned to good use.
An answer is given to those who despair at the sight of
the immense waste of the world, of the absurdity of life;
the hint of an explanation rather than an answer, for
"our view is so limited . . . of course there is no answer
here. We catch hints . . ."

God is the reason for man's existence, the only clue to
the mystery of personality. He created man in his own
image, after "his likeness", and nothing can ever blur
completely the image of God in man. It is like a birth-
mark that cannot be rubbed out; it is our true self, never
to be realized fully in time, but always present even when
concealed under superficial layers of borrowed garments.
"If God had been like a toad, you could have rid the
globe of toads, but when God was like yourself, it was no
good being content with stone figures—you had to kill
yourself among the graves." Pascal has defined the
double nature of man and his tragedy: at once an angel
and an animal, a miserable creature and yet aware of his
misery, dignified by this knowledge and endowed with an
inner sense of God: "Notwithstanding the sight of all our

miseries, which press upon us and take us by the throat, we have an instinct which we cannot repress, and which lifts us up." Man is deeply implicated in God, for it is only in him that he can find his real existence and perfect his self. There is an ontological relationship between man and God, and only in the development of this relationship can the self exist and develop and freedom be found.

Although philosophy has provided various definitions of freedom, the fact remains that it is extraordinarily difficult to define. What appears to be freedom—namely the power to choose—would be denied by modern psychology to a whole class of human beings who are in fact unable to choose. Freedom cannot be equated with free-will. But if freedom is merely the power to choose, then Greene's novels would appear to be dominated entirely by fate. His view, nevertheless, is that of the Catholic theologians who recognize no other freedom than that of accepting the vocation to which we are called by God. Paul Rostenne has analysed this concept of freedom in Greene's work with admirable clarity. What in Greene's novels is described in concrete terms as an active power deeply rooted in man's personality is simply a demonstration in fiction of the ideas expressed to-day by writers like Louis Lavelle or Gabriel Marcel. These ideas are not, however, generally stated directly in Greene's work; one has to guess at them, as one does in life, and discover the belief underlying his vision. Once the fundamental order of his world becomes apparent, we arrive at a deeper understanding and a more intimate knowledge, just as we do in the process of discovering a human being or a work of art.

While the secular element in Greene's novels is rich and true enough to hold the interest of any reader, it is only by bearing in mind and heart the Christian view of life that a reader will appreciate the profound significance of his work. God calls us to an individual vocation, but leaves us free to hurt him; and this is the very act by which we lose or degrade our freedom. We shall have to accomplish our destiny, in any case, but we can either refuse to face it and so become the victims of fate, or accept it as a vocation. Thus man's very freedom accounts for his paradoxical predicament: "Vocation, destiny," writes Paul Rostenne, "such are in fact the two poles of man's condition. Man must dedicate himself if he is not to be enchained. And Greene shows that this is the very core of the human drama. Freedom cannot be attained unless it is realized in the form of vocation."

Only the saints realize to some extent this perfecting of their being; and even for them the division resulting from sin still exists, but they carry with them the promise of the unity of our being, which comes from the total acceptance of God's love. Although perfect freedom is not found in this world, we nevertheless believe that nothing is impossible for God and that, in his infinite love, his grace never completely fails man. Man has only to seize it at the very last moment in a supreme act of freedom to be saved, for the image of God in us never forgets him who created us after his likeness.

81

*"And so faith came to one—shapelessly, without
dogma, a presence above a croquet lawn, something
associated with violence, cruelty, evil across the way.
One began to believe in heaven because one believed in
hell, but for a long while it was only hell one could
picture with a certain intimacy."*

THE LAWLESS ROADS

IN THIS REVELATION of early experience Greene once
again helps us to understand his characters more clearly.
We have already laid stress on what, in his childhood,
was an almost excessive sensitivity, a somewhat morbid
obsession with evil, transferred into his dreams and later
colouring the deepest levels of his personality as well as
his writings. Although religion, he tells us, was to explain
the childish symbols, the primary attitude is never much
modified. The first thing he imagines with any intimacy
is hell; it is the basis of belief in any spiritual world,
because only supernatural forces can be held responsible
for the unfathomable horror. And the soul can only have
an intuition of heaven when it has been purified by this
terrible vision. Conversely, the nearer the soul of man
approaches the bliss of heaven in the presence of God,
the more it suffers from the sight of evil. It is thus that
the greatest saints have to fight face to face with the
devil, that Satan appears with such intensity, for
example, in the spiritual world of Bernanos.

God's revelation to the individual man comes first as a
sense of something invaluable missing and is followed by
a certain intuition that a God exists. In the hearts of all
men, a nostalgia for the absolute works more or less
unconsciously; in moments of lucidity, we catch a glimpse

82

of a deeper reality than that ordinarily experienced in the world of right and wrong. The fundamental anxiety of man is the first and last sign of a Christian civilization: "Perhaps all we can really demand is the divided mind, the uneasy conscience, the sense of personal failure." It is because of her utter lack of the faintest feeling of this kind that Ida Arnold in *Brighton Rock* does not touch us as a real human being; she is simplified into a symbol. The same cannot be said of any of Greene's later characters, and this is one of the surest signs of his development. All those who refuse to conform—Coral Musker in *Stamboul Train*, Anthony Farrant in *England Made Me*, Conrad Drover and even the Police Commissioner in *It's a Battlefield*, Raven in *A Gun for Sale*—look in vain for another order to believe in. They move in the darkness of a limbo, with only their irrepressible religious instinct to guide them and foster their dissatisfaction, rising like the tide of nausea, in times of awareness. In Elizabeth, in *The Man Within*, the religious feeling is more definite, but not clearly linked to any specific creed. Minty (an Anglican) in *England Made Me* is claimed by a presence in the darkness of churches that draws him "more than food". Jules in *It's a Battlefield*, who is the first practising Catholic in Greene's novels, is struck by the Church's teaching on evil and sin. More significant is Dr Czinner in *Stamboul Train* who, having blown out all the candles, is overcome by a nostalgia for his former Catholicism which seems "suddenly so beautiful, as infinitely desirable and as hopelessly lost as youth". In his failure, he finds himself praying "God forgive me". He craves the forgiveness of sins, the healing blessedness of religion.

83

In the three novels with which we are concerned we are taken much further into the mystery of the spiritual personality. As we have already noted, their heroes are Catholics, openly aware of and concerned with the risk of damnation. In these novels we are introduced to the Catholic belief (further developed in *The End of the Affair*) that the sacrament is a conditioning factor in a Catholic's life, setting its seal upon him and creating him anew. Herein lies the real determinism of Pinkie, the whisky-priest and Scobie, while Helen Rolt, for instance, who is not a Catholic, is not similarly bound. "She's lucky. She's free, Wilson," Louise explains. And yet how far in fact from a real determinism this token of love is; it does not interfere with our freedom, but strengthens it with the means to develop and so helps us in our journey towards death. Pinkie, the whisky-priest and Scobie are thus 'sealed' by baptism, Scobie further by marriage, and the priest by his ordination. The Church teaches that there is always hope, even for such as these, in the act of contrition and the sacrament of penance. While they rot from the poison of their sin, the voice of their conscience is never completely stilled. The inward man, born with the grace of baptism, is a believer despite himself, however little he may justify his faith by works.

Pinkie, like everyone in Nelson Place, is a 'Roman'; he believes in hell with a religious intensity explained by the only experience he has had of life—an image of hell in this world. "Of course it's true . . . it's the only thing that fits. . . . Of course, there's hell. Flames and damnation . . . torments." Pain is the only form of eternity he can

84

conceive. The Boy's distorted face grins, as if animated by some evil supernatural force. He is a servant of the devil: "Credo in unum Satanum." There are indeed numerous references to hell or damnation in Pinkie's thoughts or conversation. The theme takes on an obsessional form when he talks to Rose, who feels by a certain quality in him that he "believes in things"; it's no use his pretending to her. But his belief, which might have become the intense faith of a saint—he had sworn to be a priest—is perverted to evil, through a complete lack of that other theological virtue, charity. And hope, too, will be found wanting. Pinkie thinks that perhaps the holy water didn't "take" when he was christened; and later we are told that his mind could not conceive of good or of heaven and that he could not take the steps required to rise above the evil surrounding him.

Pinkie, however, is aware of charity in Rose, who attracts him because in a sense she completes him, and in the old woman fumbling at her beads, "It was like the sight of damnation," but "this was not one of the damned: he watched with horrified fascination: this was one of the saved." There is another self in him, lurking in the depths of his unconscious, whose claims he cannot wholly forget and which cannot be completely denied by his superficial self. His conscience warns him that he cannot escape from life for ever or from his spiritual destiny. It is the faint call of the God of his childhood, of his choirboy days: "Dona nobis pacem", the nostalgia roused by the sound of music or by fear—"as if for something he had lost or forgotten or rejected"—"for the tiny confessional box, the priest's voice . . .", for another life from

85

which he feels excluded. In the end Pinkie is overwhelmed for a while by the emotion of "something trying to get in", bringing with it a sense of "huge havoc—the confession, the penance and the sacrament". Here again we are reminded of Greene's own experience as recorded in *Journey Without Maps*: "It is the earliest dream that I can remember . . . this dream of something outside that has got to come in. . . . This is simply power, a force exerted on a door, an influence that drifted after me upstairs and pressed against windows." Scobie also, as we shall see, has the impression, just before he dies, that "someone seeks to get in". For him as for Pinkie, this feeling takes on a religious meaning, as the ultimate manifestation of the presence of God.

But Pinkie turns out to be unfaithful to any belief but hell, a belief all the more strong on account of the intensity of his yearning (expressed in overwhelming ambition) for an absolute. Opposed to him is the resigned face of Piker, the waiter in the hotel at the end of the novel. "They were oddly alike and allusively different." Piker is one of the faithful who go to Mass on Sundays and are afraid of burning. Rose too is doomed to goodness; she does not hesitate to commit mortal sin for the sake of love, which in her eyes has a sacramental value; but because she has never ceased to believe, because of the fidelity of her devotion, she is saved at the very last moment from the horror of suicide to which she is driven by Pinkie's power over her.

Scobie, as we have already noted, brings a new complexity to Pinkie's case. He is not a Catholic by birth, but converted at the time of his marriage. Although he believes, his faith is rather a religious habit, a habit of piety than a passionate conviction transforming his life. He is one of the multitude of 'church-goers'. Prayer is a formality to be observed, like writing up his diary at night. "He closed the diary, and . . . began to pray. This also was a habit. He said the Our Father, the Hail Mary, and then . . . he added an act of contrition. It was a formality not because he felt himself free from serious sin but because it had never occurred to him that his life was important enough one way or another. He didn't drink, he didn't fornicate, he didn't even lie, but he never regarded this absence of sin as virtue. When he thought about it at all, he regarded himself as a man in the ranks, the member of an awkward squad, who had no opportunity to break the more serious military rules." Although Scobie goes to confession every month it leaves him only with a feeling of emptiness, of a routine which no longer makes sense. "I'm not sure that I even believe", he confesses to Father Rank. Louise, whose conformism supported him, has gone away; and this is the moment of crisis when temptation overcomes him and he commits adultery. "Somewhere on the face of those obscure waters moved the sense of yet another wrong and another victim, not Louise, nor Helen. Away in the town the cocks began to crow for the false dawn." With his sin is born a sense of betrayal and of desertion; but his faith is too weak to withstand the impact of his new situation.

He carries on like "the villagers on the slope of Vesuvius", at the same time sharing Pinkie's belief in

hell. "They tell us it may be a permanent sense of loss."
This is precisely how remorse works in Scobie's mind; he
has the sense of being a stranger in the country of the
faithful: "Suddenly Scobie was aware of a sense of exile.
Over there where all these people knelt, was a country to
which he would never return." At the same time, he is
stricken by a terrible awareness of the pain he is inflict-
ing on God by his degradation: "It's striking God when
he is down—in my power", he explains to Helen; and
later, before the perpetration of the sacrilegious communion: "I am the Cross, he thought, He will never
speak the word to save Himself from the Cross, but if
only wood were made so that it didn't feel, if only the
nails were senseless as people believe." After the murder
of Ali: "O God . . . I've killed you: you've served me all
these years and I've killed you at the end of them. God
lay there under the petrol drums and Scobie felt the
tears in his mouth, salt in the cracks of his lips. You
served me and I did this to you. You were faithful to me,
and I wouldn't trust you."

God now takes on in his eyes the full reality of a person. In passing, it is worth noting the difference in the intensity of his religious sense before and after his sin. His
prayer rises to God in the simple terms of his pain. He
converses with him directly: "O God convince me, help
me, convince me. Make me feel that I am more important than that child. . . . Make me put my own soul
first. Give me trust in your mercy to the one I abandon."
He fails again and again, but in the end the voice of God
is heard speaking to Scobie through his conscience "from
the cave of his body". He is the inner critic, whispering

words of love to the lost desperate soul, trying to bring it back to him, "as if the sacrament which had lodged there for his damnation gave tongue. You say you love me, and yet you'll do this to me—rob me of you for ever. I made you with love. I've wept your tears. I've saved you from more than you will ever know; I planted in you this longing for peace only so that one day I could satisfy your longing and watch your happiness. And now you push me away, you put me out of your reach. There are no capital letters to separate us when we talk together. I am not Thou but simply you, when you speak to me; I am humble as any other beggar. Can't you trust me as you'd trust a faithful dog? I have been faithful to you for two thousand years." God in his love never forces himself upon us: "Dear God, forget me, but the weak fingers kept their feeble pressure. He had never known before so clearly the weakness of God." Scobie's ultimate fault is to believe that his sin is too great for God to forgive it. He cannot trust to the mercy of God. "It is not Grace that has failed him but he who has failed to believe in Grace." In the suicidal darkness, a presence is felt, which is very likely God's. "It seemed to him as though someone outside the room was seeking him, calling him and he made a last effort to indicate that he was here."

The whisky-priest, for all his failures and his sins, is, as we have seen, faithful to the essential; he never ceases to believe in God's mercy and love and in the eternal character of his priesthood. He is overwhelmed by the sense that his own inadequacy does not hinder the flow of divine grace through his hands to those to whom he

89

ministers. Padre José is also aware of being a priest for ever, but he throws up the sponge, while the whisky-priest carries on with his mission. Even though he is in a state of mortal sin, he is still the man who brings the body of God to the abandoned people: "It doesn't matter so much my being a coward—and all the rest. I can put God into a man's mouth just the same—and I can give him God's pardon. It wouldn't make any difference to that if every priest in the Church was like me." The presence of God is paradoxically what the bad priest stands for in the abandoned land; and this knowledge keeps him there. All his former pride has left him. He is humbled by the sense of his own inadequacy.

The faith of the whisky-priest is reduced to a sense of mystery. This at least is a truly religious sense, for even if faith involves intellectual knowledge, it also needs the participation of man's whole being. Cut off from sacramental life, something fundamental of his faith survives. "The simple ideas of hell and heaven moved in his brain: life without books, without contact with educated men, had peeled away from his memory everything but the simplest outline of the mystery." Instead of books, he has men and he has learned to love them with that charity without which faith cannot subsist. For every man is the image of God and the whisky-priest knows it; Christ has died even for Judas and for a world which too often stirs our hearts with nausea and yet with pity too. "When you visualized a man or woman carefully, you could always begin to feel pity . . . that was a quality God's image carried with it." Like Scobie the whisky-priest is painfully aware of his sins but does not seem

90

able to make an act of contrition; like Scobie he cannot repent the love and does not distinguish his sin from the far from condemnable love he feels for his child. What ultimately saves him from despair is his deep humility. Whatever he finally does to answer God's call is not, he knows, the result of a voluntary choice; but who can judge how valuable this mere act of acceptance appears in the eyes of God? The whisky-priest after all has never failed to trust him in his hidden purpose of salvation and love. With God all things are possible: "If God intended him to escape, he could snatch him away in front of a firing squad." God is merciful, he knows, and in the end his private anxieties are put aside. "He felt only an immense disappointment because he had to go to God empty-handed, with nothing at all." The regret of having so nearly missed sanctity is the light poured into his heart at the last minute.

Each of us has been given, however unevenly, a share of this light. Our part is to be faithful, as our conscience directs us, and to orientate our lives accordingly and not to be found wanting. We have no right to judge the fidelity of others, because we do not know what their share has been. Greene's heroes are undoubtedly poor in human and spiritual gifts; but we know that God never fails even his most abject creatures. Pinkie in his black heart is still moved by a recollection of his spiritual dependence on God and by a sense of loss. Scobie shares this sense of loss with an added awareness of the pain inflicted on God. The priest at least has overcome pride, which is the downfall of Pinkie and Scobie, and he at least is capable of a certain degree of detachment and of loving consent to God's will. He knows that to love God is to "protect Him from oneself".

III   THE SPIRITUAL PATTERN WROUGHT
                    THROUGH HISTORY

> *"We really want what He wants, we really want,*
> *though we do not know it, our pain, our suffering and*
> *our solitude, while we think that we only want our*
> *pleasure. We think that we dread death and run away*
> *from it, while we really want our death as He wanted*
> *His. . . . He dies again with each dying man. We want*
> *all that He wants but we do not know that we want it,*
> *we do not know ourselves, we shall retire into ourselves*
> *only when we die, and there He will be waiting for us."*
>
> George Bernanos

THE WHISKY-PRIEST KNOWS that God's love burns. "God is love. I don't say the heart doesn't feel a taste of it but what a taste. The smallest glass of love mixed with a pint pot of ditch-water. We wouldn't recognize *that* love. It might even look like hate. It would be enough to scare us—God's love. It set fire to a bush in the desert, didn't it, and smashed open graves and set the dead walking in the dark. Oh, a man like me would run a mile to get away if he felt that love around." This fire awakens not only the longing lodged deep in man's heart; God, who knows the weakness of his people, is constantly working to bring back the unfaithful. This theme is recurrent in the Bible. God's guidance of his people through history is applicable to the individual human soul. Each of us in one way or another is given up to "whoredoms", and God in his jealousy or infinite love

92

chastises us for our unfaithfulness. God is not resigned to our sins and tries to strip us of our false, superficial self, in order to lead us where we really want to be, though we may not know it, blinded as we are by sin. God teaches us while he punishes us. The trials sent to the Hebrews were not only an atonement for their sins but also a lesson of humility and love; God's ultimate purpose is to force each of his children to find freedom in a new heart and a new spirit during their progress through life. Life is granted to us so that we may co-operate in the universal process of salvation. This is "the real web of our life, the spiritual web which may be seen, when we look carefully, through the more or less intricate pattern of the temporal", as Julian Green has said. God's secret purpose appears thus to be the key to the "territory without maps", the thread guiding us through the "labyrinthine ways", the solution to the child's dissected map—those fragmentary pieces which show themselves as essential parts of the whole. Claude-Edmonde Magny has pointed out the importance of every single detail in the detective element in Greene's novels. In the same way every detail counts in the spiritual pattern woven into the lives of his characters. "It was just possible", the whisky-priest thought, "that a year without anxiety might save this man's soul. You only had to turn up the underside of any situation and out came scuttling these small absurd contradictory situations. He had given way to despair—and out of that had emerged a human soul and love—not the best love, but love all the same." It is worth while analysing some of the spiritual experiences of these characters, some stages of the journey backwards to the interior

93

self and ultimately to death, when we at last are restored to our true selves and we find God awaiting us.

Greene reminds us of how impotent we are towards our own and other people's unhappiness. Pinkie was driven to revolt by the terrible experiences of his childhood; Scobie was stupefied by the misery that tormented everyone he loved; the whisky-priest himself was the most wretched of the victims of the evil spirit devastating his country. Like all Greene's characters they are crushed, as it were, between gigantic hands. From the darkness there arises a cry of lamentation which awakens in us an awareness of our miserable situation. Greene is obsessed by the idea that happy people are either ignorant or selfish. Avoiding the sight of pain, or shutting their eyes to it, they deny reality. For suffering is the necessary price of evil and evil is still the way of the world.

The Crucifixion, however, gives a new value to suffering. Its relation to the growth of man's spiritual self is one of the fundamental themes of Christian thought, one of the ontological aspects of the human condition. "Man has places in his heart which do not yet exist, and into them enters suffering in order that they may have existence", writes Léon Bloy. Berdyaev, also, in *Spirit and Reality*, underlines this close relationship in terms which can properly be applied to Greene's vision. "In this world, spirituality ever preserves its connection with the experience of suffering, with the contradictions and conflicts of human existence, with the hostile facts of death and eternity. A sensitive awareness of evil and a capacity for suffering are one of the attributes of the

94

spiritual man." Our miseries and all the obstacles we meet in our path must be regarded not as the mere actualization of fate but as problems to be solved for the development of our spiritual personality, as a trial of the capacity of our interior strength to assert itself, and as a way of self-liberation. "A spiritual attitude to suffering implies illumination, or a vital knowledge of the meaning of suffering and a sense of liberation. The development of spirituality is a sure sign that man has not been crushed by suffering. The acceptance of the Cross is at the same time an alleviation of suffering, for it assumes a purpose in the spiritual life." We are no longer alone. Sarah in *The End of the Affair*, kissing the birthmark on Smythe's cheek, thinks: "I am kissing pain and pain belongs to You as happiness never does. I love You in Your pain. . . . How good You are. You might have killed us with happiness, but You let us be with You in pain." Not only does the experience of suffering deepen our being, but it also opens our heart to the outside world.

But we do not know that we really want pain and solitude and death. We are reluctant to undertake the ever-repeated and painful task of achieving our own grown-up personality by a continuous fidelity; we try to avoid opening our hearts to the miseries about us, we do not like being disturbed in our quiet ivory towers, we are afraid to have to mourn over the Passion of Christ. We are easily contented with cheap satisfactions and allured by evil ways. We are perpetually postponing the disturbing moment of awareness. Jacques Rivière writes: "A man is nothing so long as he does not begin to consider himself as nothing. . . . This is the only important thing: to get away from oneself." But we lack the courage for that. God in his zeal will then try us by stripping us of our superficialities, our sensualities, all that obstructs the way to perfect love. In the Scriptures and in the writings of the mystics we see how God drives us into the spiritual conflict raging in the desolation of the desert. He will discover the nakedness of the unfaithful soul, take away from her all the gifts with which he had enriched her. Then in a complete abandonment and solitude he will "allure her and bring her into the wilderness, and speak comfortably unto her". In the desert Christ overcame Satan; in the desert, in the spiritual death to his old self, man will be purified from his sins and atone for them; and when he has been brought to a state of complete humility, God will plead with him face to face.

One cannot help feeling how naturally Greene's spiritual knowledge is transferred into his books. These men whom we have seen completely disintegrated by sin appear at the same time to be closer to spiritual reality than the ignorant innocent or the pious complacent. Greene is obsessed by the truth affirmed by Léon Bloy in *La Femme Pauvre* and by Péguy: "Le pécheur est au coeur même de chrétienté . . . nul n'est aussi compétent que le pécheur en matière de chrétienté. Nul, si ce n'est le saint." Of Pinkie himself, however hopeless his case seems to be, it can at least be said that he was never satisfied with life and always refused to compromise. Moreover he had more than an average share of suffering and was broken, in all his human desires or repulsions, by God's anger against his infernal pride. True, he had perceived a tiny

96

crack in the Brighton walls by which he could be saved, but the darkness of his ways through the world made it difficult for him to become fully conscious of the light. Did the feeble voice of the mysterious presence in him finally succeed in making itself heard during his fall from the cliff edge to the sea?

Scobie's spiritual self reaches the conscious level. From relative indifference he comes to awareness of that self. Through sin he develops a sense of loss and of nakedness. God tries to bring back the soul by withdrawing until the soul says: "I will go and return to my first husband; for then was it better with me than now." But Scobie's eyes are blinded and he fails to follow the impulse of his conscience which is a longing for peace in God. He is brought to a place of desolation where nothing is left of the old Scobie, where loneliness seats itself beside him. "He felt as though he had exiled himself so deeply in the desert that his skin had taken on the colour of the sand." He seems alone with his sin; but loneliness happens to have a voice and that voice is the voice of God pleading with him; solitude happens to be a presence and it is the presence of God. We are struck by this intimate contact of the soul with its God, alone with him before the ultimate act.

The case of the priest shows more clearly the spiritual enrichment that may follow the ordeal of life and sin. His nakedness, too, is uncovered; he is gradually deprived of the resources of his old life, until the last memory of it—the small ball of paper he drops before being caught by the police—is also taken away, and he has nothing left. He endures hunger, solitude, fever; he has to overcome fear in order to carry on. He too feels abandoned and deserted; and in this desolation he is too weak to resist temptation. But in his corruption he is saved from his own pride and discovers love. In the prison cell he experiences a strange communion with those who are suffering like him, before being led through a kind of limbo, as a last stage of purification; even Coral, the child of whom he expected so much, is taken away. "He had passed into a region of abandonment—almost as if he had died [in the cell] with the old man's head on his shoulder and now wandered in a kind of limbo, because he wasn't good or bad enough." There God will speak to him through the faith of the Indian woman with whom he travels across the desolate plateau. His short stay on the other side of the border is another kind of limbo where in his weakness he learns humility once more; he is ready then to accept martyrdom instead of continuing his life of sin. From Greene himself we know he is convinced that the fundamental paradox of Christianity lies in the co-existence of good and evil. The temptation in the wilderness has a sacramental value for man. The Belgian priest, Father Damien, in the leper-hospital of Molokai in Honolulu, was not so different from the whisky-priest. Sarah Miles herself in *The End of the Affair* would meet with her God in the desert which she vainly tried to fill with her love for Bendrix. Thus God breaks the heart of man; for the sacrifices of God are a broken spirit.

*"Now . . . having loved His own which were in the
world Jesus loved them unto the end."*

St John

*"The efficacity of the divine blood is such that a single
true impulse of charity, however imperceptible, may in
the scales of divine justice balance thousands of
crimes."*

Léon Bloy

LOVE IS THE final answer to evil, the unity for which we
must strive, the ultimate victory of God. Even if our love
is mixed with a lot of ditch water, the faintest portion of
true love in the mixture is worth more than all those
achievements which are actuated only by an egotistic
impulse. If the apparent quality of our love varies, it at
least comes from the same source; and the smallest act
of true love wrung from the weakest man may, according
to his nature, be as valuable as the act of the greatest
saint in God's eyes. He alone can penetrate our deepest
intentions.

We are not told explicitly of any evidence of Pinkie's
capacity for love. But with Rose we meet for the first
time the theme of the supreme sacrifice, offered to God
for the love and salvation of men, which in the other
novels will take the extreme form of the whisky-priest's
martyrdom and Scobie's oblation. Péguy seems to have
influenced Greene profoundly during the period when
these three novels were being written and it provides an
additional link between them. "He was a good man, a
holy man, and he lived in sin all through his life, because
he couldn't bear the idea that any soul could suffer dam-

99

nation. . . . This man decided that if any soul was going to be damned, he would be damned too. He never took the sacraments, he never married his wife in church. I don't know, my child, but some people think he was—well, a saint. I think he died in what we are told is mortal sin—I'm not sure: it was in the war: perhaps. . . . It was a case of greater love hath no man than this that he lay down his soul for his friend." This is how the old priest tries to comfort Rose in her desperate love and mourning for Pinkie. She does not want to be parted from him for eternity; she is sorry not to have killed herself with him: "I want to be like him—damned." In her exclusive love she has a sense of her responsibility towards him; when she links her destiny with his she knows in her heart it has to be for ever, for better and for worse; for love of him she commits mortal sin by marrying without the sacrament; for him she is ready to give everything, even life itself. "Wasn't it better", thought Arthur Rowe in *The Ministry of Fear*, "to take part even in the crimes of people you loved, if it was necessary hate as they did, and if that were the end of everything suffer damnation with them rather than be saved alone?" But Rose is miraculously saved from the horror of suicide. After Pinkie had gone, "she would have found the courage to kill herself if she hadn't been afraid that somewhere in that obscure countryside of death they might miss each other—mercy operating somehow for one and not for the other."

The whisky-priest sacrifices himself to the people he serves. Once complacent and successful, he discovers love in his degradation. "That was another mystery: it sometimes seemed to him that venial sins—impatience, an unimportant lie, pride, a neglected opportunity—cut you off from grace more completely than the worst sins of all. Then, in his innocence, he had felt no love for anyone: now in his corruption he had learnt . . ." His heart has been opened to love—the love of God and an "enormous tenderness" for the image of God. There he is with the peons adding to their daily suffering, the hostages dying for him, the thieves in the prison, the old man whose head lies sideways against his shoulder, and for whom he consents to be made a little uncomfortable, the Indian woman for whose sake he climbs back towards the plateau, the American whose photograph is hanging with his on the police station wall, like the two thieves at the Cross, and even the half-caste, Judas. "Christ had died for this man too: how could he pretend with his pride and lust and cowardice to be any more worthy of that death than this half-caste?" Above all he feels bound by his love for his daughter, the living, ugly testimony of his sin, towards whom he feels an enormous responsibility. She fills his unconscious thoughts and is with him in his dreams. When he dreams of her, he prays: "O God help her. Damn me; I deserve it, but let her live for ever." In his humility he never allows himself to condemn any of those children to whom he has been sent; for himself only, aware of his corruption, he can conceive damnation. "I do know this—that if there's ever been a single man in this state damned, then I'll be damned too." And he finally accomplishes the greatest act of love, to lay down his life for God and his beloved.

Marcel Moré has analysed how love secretly burns in

the soul of the neurotic and the sinner, and how its light will lead him to find his freedom and his spiritual self in the darkness of sin among the ruins of the other superficial self. Moré and Evelyn Waugh have questioned whether Scobie's fault could not be considered as a loving sacrifice. Scobie's two oblations are those of peace and damnation, the first leading logically to the second. Scobie, by offering his peace for the child who dies in his arms with its face convulsed ("like a navvy's with labour"), passes from pity to the purest love. "Father", he prayed, "give her peace. Take away my peace for ever, but give her peace." Scobie gives away the very peace he longs to attain. Marcel Moré writes about this sacrifice: "If Scobie does not offer his own will on the altar, he at least gives away to God what then . . . represents his most precious property, this rather miserable peace which is 'his', but which he has bought at such a high price." Greene himself replied in a letter to Moré: "Obviously one did have in mind that when he offered up his peace for the child it was genuine prayer and had the results that followed. I always believe that such prayers, though obviously a God would not fulfil them to the limit of robbing him of a peace for ever, are answered up to a point as a kind of test of a man's sincerity and to see whether in fact the offer was one merely based on emotion." Scobie's prayer is heard. The torment of seeing those he loves suffer, the horror of striking God, of being only a source of death and pain will not be spared him.

Scobie is thus led to his second oblation. He has lost hope; all he has left is the exploration of the "territory of despair". During Mass, before his sacrilege, he is a

102

prey to tragic anxiety; he suffers pangs of agony: "Pax, pacis, pacem: all the declinations of the word 'peace' drummed on his ears through the Mass. He thought: I have left even the hope of peace for ever." And later: "With open mouth (the time had come) he made one last attempt at prayer, 'O God, I offer up my damnation to you. Take it. Use it for them,' and was aware of the pale papery taste of his eternal sentence on the tongue."

In the darkness before death, which Greene conjures up for the first time, "between the stirrup and the ground", the same interior self which was still capable of offering his peace and his damnation answers to a supreme call. "And automatically at the call of need, at the cry of a victim, Scobie strung himself to act. He dredged his consciousness up from an infinite distance in order to make some reply. He said aloud, 'Dear God, I love!' . . ." This prayer, the last impulse of life, is all the more moving for the imminence of death; it is purposely left unfinished and hence ambiguous, but it was undoubtedly a genuine act of love. Father Rank adds the comforting epilogue: "It may seem an odd thing to say— when a man's as wrong as he was—but I think, from what I saw of him, that he really loved God." Most valuable are Greene's explanations, in the letter to Marcel Moré quoted above, of what he intended by Scobie's last prayer: "My own intention was to make it completely vague as to whether he was expressing his love for the two women or his love for God. My own feeling about this character is that he was uncertain himself and that was why the thing broke off. The point I would like to make is that at the moment of death even an

103

expression of sexual love comes within the borders of charity. After all, when a man knows that he is dying in a few moments, sexual love itself becomes completely altruistic—pride can no longer enter into it, nor can the hope of receiving or giving pleasure; it is love pure and simple, and therefore, there must be some confusion in the mind as to the object of love."

Thus Greene seems to credit Rose, the whisky-priest and Scobie, for all their sinfulness, with spiritual experiences comparable with those which are generally reserved for the saints. Moses prays to God for the people who have sinned in the desert: "Yet now, if thou wilt, forgive their sin; and if not, blot me, I pray thee, out of thy book which thou hast written." And St Paul, mourning over the destiny of his brothers, the Hebrews: "I could wish that myself were accursed from Christ for my brethren." This is not the first time we have underlined the relationship, suggested by Greene (who follows here the Christian tradition), between the sinner and the saint, and its connection with the single source of spiritual life and love. We have also detected in Greene's characters, even in the whisky-priest's martyrdom, symptoms of masochism in the instinct leading them to escape by self-destruction, and in their obsession with suffering. But we cannot estimate the exact proportions of the morbid, or even neurotic impulse, and of pure love implied in their supreme act. This is known only to God, who uses and sanctifies our natural tendencies with his grace when we abandon ourselves to his will. We think with emotion of all those who struggle against all possible forms of neurosis, and who, like a Paule Régnier, yielding to the fascination of suicide, still love where they betray.

One of the greatest mysteries of the spiritual world is the communion of all men in evil and in good, the communion of saints and sinners—for we are never alone, as the whisky-priest knew. We share responsibility for our sins, as we also share love; our destiny is linked with that of other men, not only physically by relation of blood or social environment, but by deeper, mysterious spiritual bonds. Therein lies a hint of an explanation of the horror, of the apparent waste and suffering in the world, and especially of innocent children who play such an important part in the lives of Pinkie, the whisky-priest and Scobie. One soul can atone for another, and by suffering and love lift the load weighing on its freedom.

The point is explicitly raised at the end of *Brighton Rock*, when Pinkie dimly perceives that Rose, with her faith in him and her love, might be the means of his salvation. Her sacrifice will not be wasted; she has assumed for herself responsibility for Pinkie's soul. Who knows how much her love will weigh? And then she carries within her body the promise of life. The child she believes she has conceived will atone anew for his father: " 'With your simplicity and his force. . . . Make him a saint—to pray for his father.' A sudden feeling of immense gratitude broke through the pain—it was as if she had been given the sight a long way off of life going on again."

This spiritual relationship is still more apparent in *The Power and the Glory*. The destiny of the whisky-priest is linked not only with that of the faithful people who teach

105

him love, and the murderers with whom he is associated, but more closely with that of his own daughter according to the flesh, for whose sake he wants to offer himself up. Even more mysterious is the bond which ties him to the child at the banana-station, his daughter according to the spirit, whom in a sense he brings to spiritual life. Coral, the pure adolescent who meets with a violent death a few weeks after she awakes to maturity, ministers to the priest in his dreams, as she did in life: "The glass by his plate began to fill with wine, and looking up he saw that the child from the banana-station was serving him" . . . and then "the taps began. . . . He asked, 'What is it?' 'News,' the child said, watching him with a stern, responsible and interested gaze." A code to what language, a password to what territory, news from what world? The dead do not abandon us. Coral comes to comfort the priest before he passes from this world into eternity. His long apparently useless service in the godless state is given a greater significance, when the new priest appears after his death. The whisky-priest did not know that he was a necessary link in the chain and that God would not cease to be present in the dark territory after his own life had ended.

In *The Heart of the Matter*, the same impression of spiritual solidarity is conveyed. Scobie's sacrifice, or at least his intense suffering from the pain inflicted on those he loves by the treachery of the world or by his own impotence, appears to be not altogether vain. The dying child in Pende for whom he offers his peace will find eternal rest as she repeats after him the word of trust and comfort: "Father". After his death, Helen, who is

106

little more than a child, too, is left with a vacant place in her heart that needs to be filled. "Do you believe in a God?" she asks Bagster, and exclaims: "I wish I did . . . I wish I did." And later: "She was alone again in the darkness behind her lids, and the wish struggled in her body like a child: her lips moved, but all she could think of to say was, 'For ever and ever, Amen' . . ." Scobie's love and death have cleared the way in her. Another face, that of a pious child dressed in white muslin, who had died three years before far away, is invisibly but nevertheless intensely present. "A wife shares too much of a man's sin for perfect love; but a daughter may save him at the last", the Portuguese captain had written to his daughter in the letter which Scobie opened. Catherine's spirit was present at the death of the other child in Pende to urge her father to an act of pure charity. And she reminds us of another pious girl who pleads for her father on her death-bed—Marie, in François Mauriac's *Noeud de Vipères*, who opens in the dark and passionate soul of her avaricious father a gap through which the flame of love will issue to transform him: "By this bed . . . the secret of life and death has been given to me. . . . A little girl was dying for me."

When all is said and done, Greene leaves us on a note of hope and optimism, as the infinite calm of death spreads its silence over the place where a man has lived and sinned—but also loved and died. God's mercy, even if it sometimes looks like punishment, has no limits. Pascal exclaimed: "I would know how this animal, who knows himself to be so weak, has the right to measure the mercy of God, and set limits to it, suggested by his own fancy." Greene, following him, insists on the fact that we have no right to set up as judges in this matter. The nameless priest says to Rose: "You can't conceive, my child, nor can I or anyone the appalling strangeness of the mercy of God." And Father Rank to Louise: "For goodness' sake, Mrs Scobie, don't imagine you—or I—know a thing about God's mercy." And the whisky-priest: "I don't know a thing about the mercy of God." The light of the infinite love of God is shed over all Greene's characters. Nowhere in the Scriptures is there a text that directly states that any man is consigned to the torments of Hell. What we do know with certainty is that the thief crucified with Jesus, probably no better human material than Greene's characters, was the first to whom the joy of heaven was promised. "Hell is not of this world", says the priest of Bernanos's *Journal d'un Curé de Campagne*, "the lowest of human beings, even though he no longer thinks he can love, still has in him the power of loving. Our very hate is resplendent, and the least tormented of the fiends would warm himself in what we call our despair, as in a morning of brilliant sunshine. Hell is not to love any more." There is even a chance for a Pinkie, for God is Love, and everything is mysteriously used to reveal the greatness of his Power and his Glory.

"THERE IS THE corruption of nature and there is the omnipotence of Grace; there is the misery of man, who is nothing, even in evil, and that mysterious love which takes possession of him at the very bottom of his ridiculous misery and ludicrous shame to make of him a saint and a martyr." Thus François Mauriac characterizes the situation of the whisky-priest in his preface to the French edition of *The Power and the Glory*. For Father Robert du Parc he is "neither saint nor damned but a very poor man, whom Christ has rescued, and who by his situation has been made an authentic martyr". The same question is raised about Scobie. Is he damned? Is he a saint? Is he saved? We are not sure even about Pinkie, in spite of the horror. In *Brighton Rock* Greene repeatedly and purposely refers to the old epitaph:

> "*Between the stirrup and the ground*
> *He mercy asked and mercy found.*"

Here again we wonder: is he damned, is he saved?

The very fact that such questions should be raised at all, that every attempt at a synthesis is either vain or an over-simplification, is a sign of the depth and complexity of Greene's characters. What he offers us is a tragic vision of man's predicament. The fatality of evil, the power of Grace—both forces are at war within him; he is torn between the opposed forces of his natural desires and the exigences of his inner self—the "man within". Greene's art lies in his remarkable ability to

109

reveal simultaneously man's dual nature. St Paul, Pascal and Newman before him had denounced the painful division of man's being. Greene realizes it in terms of fiction. He excels in showing the parallel progress of the fallen man and the redeemed soul, and the process by which evil and love inter-penetrate human mediocrity.

In the three novels we have been discussing there is a progressive increase of skill. In *Brighton Rock*, the conflict is dimly revealed in Pinkie himself and does not reach the level of consciousness. Rose, a minor character who nevertheless appears to complete Pinkie, is more in the line of Greene's later characters. There is still too much symbolization in this first handling of the general theme of the trilogy; in somewhat simplified terms, Pinkie is evil, Rose is good, while Ida is "nothing". The theme is too explicit and does not always blend satisfactorily with the action. But the main ideas are already there—the dichotomy in the mind, the disintegration by sin, the inner call of love in the abandonment of the desert, the continuous working of men and women on one another, and the sacrifice of life which is given its full significance in the light of the communion of all souls, the inevitable issue of death and the limitless mercy of God. In fact little more will be added to the intellectual content of Greene's vision. But *Brighton Rock*, besides being for Greene the "moment of crystallization when the dominant theme is plainly expressed, when the private universe becomes visible", is also important in its own right for its compassionate treatment of the theme of "lost childhood". *The Power and the Glory* and *The Heart of the Matter* deal with grown-up men.

In *The Power and the Glory* the conflict comes into the open in the sinful priest. We do not witness directly the process of his degradation; when we first meet him he has already reached the bottom. It is through his own thoughts and his remorseful conscience that we are able to reconstruct the past; but the labyrinthine ways of love are seen more clearly as they penetrate his soul until it is finally abandoned to the Power of God for his Glory.

The greater ambiguity and confusion of Scobie's character result from the merging of the two themes of sin and redemption to the point of bringing about the extreme paradox. The progress of sin and love in Scobie can be traced back through an equally logical chain of argument. He is the perfect illustration of how the pendulum swings between two extremes, only to be stopped by death.

Pinkie, the whisky-priest and Scobie are at one in their fundamental terror of life, in their incurable weakness and lack of will, which account for their sensitivity to their environment and for their failure. All three have a more than ordinary knowledge of evil, have felt its dangerous fascination, its indelible burn (symbolized by Pinkie's vitriol) and its annihilating power. But even Greene's feeblest creatures are free. We have seen how the possibility of an act of sublime love (however worthless it may appear at first sight) is not denied them, even if their inner self has to wait for death for its release. And yet God's works are not completed in them; the whisky-priest realized at the end that "there was only one thing that counted—to be a saint". The failure to be a saint, to surrender oneself entirely to the Grace of God, to be

111

transformed by it, to attain to one's full personality in a total faith in him, to put oneself beyond the grasp of fate by assuming one's place in time and society, and one's nature in the light of one's vocation—such shortcomings are common to all of us, and not only to Pinkie, the whisky-priest and Scobie.

We nevertheless feel a certain uneasiness at finding that none of these characters seems capable of being at one with his deeper self, or realizing the inner vision in this life. They have lost their way in the dark. Even Sarah Miles, in *The End of the Affair*, although she has made a voluntary "leap", cannot outlive the tension created in her by the conflict between her faith and her overwhelming love for Bendrix. Faith, instead of orientating their natures, seems to work against them. But the clue to their problem might well be conveyed in the words of Bernanos: "It is easier than one thinks to hate oneself. True grace is to forget oneself. Yet if all pride could die in us, the supreme grace would be to love oneself in complete humility—as any of the suffering members of Christ." Only in a humble acceptance of oneself can peace be found. The whisky-priest, in his humility, is on the verge of this discovery; when the trap closed irrevocably, "the oddest thing of all was that he felt quite cheerful. . . . He began to whistle a tune—something he had heard somewhere once." Sarah also would know some moments of this peace and supernatural joy. In *The Living Room*, the crippled priest is given a new aim in his apparently useless life through a humble recognition of his tragic powerlessness to help the young girl. His eyes are opened by her death and in the end he

112

conveys, like the priest in 'The Hint of an Explanation', an impression of serenity achieved in the loving contemplation of human suffering and the growing awareness that love and faith alone can save us.

We must bear in mind that Greene himself has stated that "the novelist's task is to draw his own likeness to any human being, the guilty as much as the innocent". And he has not yet said the last word. He seems to respond to life 'cum timore et tremore'. Like Kierkegaard, he knows that the faith of Abraham and Mary did not free them from its hardship, for "neither of them became greater than a hero by being exempt from distress and dread and the paradox: only through these tribulations did they become great." Greene's characters share his own continuous agony of mind, which must be endured by all who feel torn between a natural need for a minimum of human happiness and the exacting demands of faith. "How can life on a border be other than restless?" It is true to say that Pinkie, the whisky-priest and Scobie are tied to their particularly painful situations; it is also true that even the most wretched man is called upon to use his freedom, however far he may have to go to restore his inner self to life. Greene's vision of escape is eschatological. Only in death will the so much longed-for peace be found, in the presence of God. "Blessed are they that mourn: for they shall be comforted." Yet, it was also said: "Rejoice in the Lord always and again I say, rejoice." Pascal knew that Jesus would be in agony even to the end of the world, but he also exclaimed "Joy, Joy, tears of Joy". The tears wept at the Passion turn into the "exsultet" of the Resurrection. Greene has not yet

113

reached in his writings the peace and the unity found in complete surrender to Love, in the knowledge that the prince of this world is already defeated.

Greene invites us to meditate on our own destiny, offering us not cases to solve and classify but the mystery of people like Pinkie or Scobie or the nameless whisky-priest who cross our paths in real life. He opens our eyes (and our hearts) to the miseries around us to which we are too often blind; he tells us that, while the rejects of society, the lawless ones of this world, may need our particular love in order to rise above a tragic situation, it is not in our power to show them the way to happiness.

Greene's message is one of humility and of respect for what is a private matter between the individual soul and its creator. We realize suddenly that we know after all next to nothing about Pinkie, the whisky-priest and Scobie. Only God knows what goes on in a single human heart. Greene teaches us not to judge. He looks beyond ethics and beyond the Law, intent only on Love and the sin against Love. "These characters," he says, "are not my creation but God's. They have an eternal destiny. They are not merely playing a part for the reader's amusement. They are souls whom Christ died to save."

BIBLIOGRAPHY

Novels and Entertainments

The Man Within—1929
The Name of Action—1930
Rumour at Nightfall—1931
Stamboul Train—1932
It's a Battlefield—1934
England Made Me—1935
A Gun for Sale—1936
BRIGHTON ROCK—1938
The Confidential Agent—1939
THE POWER AND THE GLORY—1940
The Ministry of Fear—1943
THE HEART OF THE MATTER—1948
The Third Man—1950
The Fallen Idol—1950
The End of the Affair—1951

Short Stories

The Basement Room and Other Stories—1935 (reprinted
as *Nineteen Stories*—1947)
'The Hint of an Explanation'—*The Month*—Feb., 1949

Poetry

Babbling April—1925

Drama

The Living Room—1953

Travel

Journey Without Maps—1936
The Lawless Roads—1939

Essays, Etc.

The Old School—1934. Edited with an Introduction and an Essay by Graham Greene.

The Lost Childhood and Other Essays—1951

Why Do I Write? (with Elizabeth Bowen and V. S. Pritchett)—1948

Speech to the Grande Conférence Catholique at Brussels—*La Table Ronde*—Feb., 1948

Speech to the Centre Catholique des Intellectuels Français—*Foi en Jésus-Christ et Monde d'Aujourd'hui* —1949

'Les Paradoxes du Christianisme'—*Dieu Vivant*, no. XVIII

———

Critical Studies

Graham Greene, by Jacques Madaule—1949

Graham Greene Témoin des Temps Tragiques, by Paul Rostenne—1949

The Art of Graham Greene, by K. Allott and M. Farris —1951